The Story of the Grail

CHRESTIEN DE TROYES

The Story of the Grail

TRANSLATED BY

ROBERT WHITE LINKER

Chapel Hill

THE UNIVERSITY OF NORTH CAROLINA PRESS

PRINTED BY THE SEEMAN PRINTERY, DURHAM, N. C.

To

Two Spiritual Descendants
of Count Philip of Flanders
My Very Good Friends
CELESTE and EUGENE HARTLEY

Preface

THIS, the first English translation of the *Story of the Grail*, is here presented in a new edition, following a small offset printing in 1952 limited to a hundred copies. The Old French text I have used is that edited by Alfons Hilka.

I have tried to present Chrestien's work as faithfully as possible, without any false archaisms which many translators feel compelled to insert to remind the reader that the work is from the Middle Ages. Written in the twelfth century, the story has numerous mediaeval features of its own, such as inversions and shifts of tenses sometimes startling to the modern reader. I could easily have reconciled these with modern standards, but I have chosen not to do so, because they are as much a part of the author's style as is his rather lean choice of words. The story is more important than the way it is told, both in the original and in my translation. The chapter titles and running heads have been supplied by the translator, who also divided the long continuous poem into chapter-length sections for greater ease in reading.

Footnotes and other scholarly apparatus have been dispensed with in the belief that the serious student will not need them, and the general reader, seeking mainly literary and historical values, will be able to follow the rapid narrative of this English translation with greater ease and enjoyment. At the end of the text, readers will find a brief, informal listing of important texts and critical studies. The literature on the Grail in its various versions is far too vast to cover in this book. So is the question of the origin of the Grail, and that of the identity of

Arthur. I have tried only to give the interested reader something to start with. I have undoubtedly omitted the favorite references of some scholars, but the books I do list have bibliographies that will cover these omissions.

The interested reader will find on the first page of each section a footnote giving the line numbers of that portion of *Li Contes del Graal* translated in the chapter.

R.W.L.

Chapel Hill, N. C.
1960

Contents

Introduction

CHRESTIEN de Troyes, the most important writer of twelfth-century France, gives us the first purely literary treatment of King Arthur. Before Chrestien, Arthur appears only in a succession of chronicles such as those of Nennius, Geoffrey of Monmouth, Gaimar, Wace, and Layamon. Each of these writers makes his own addition to the growing legend of Arthur. Wace, for example, is the first to introduce the Round Table. It is Chrestien, however, who transfers this material to the field of literature as opposed to history, expands and develops it, and furnishes a major source and models for one of the great bodies of western literature, the Arthurian Romance. It is to Chrestien that we owe the character of Lancelot and, more especially, the theme generally known as the Holy Grail.

We have no definite biographical information on Chrestien de Troyes. Only his works remain. Two of these bear dedications, one to Marie de Champagne and one to Philip of Flanders, which enable us to date his literary activity roughly between the years 1150 and 1190. Beyond this, much has been written by inference from these two dedications, including supposedly exact dates for each of his works.

In his *Cligés*, Chrestien gives us a partial list of his writings. He says:

"He who wrote of Erec and of Enid, and put into the Romance tongue the Commands of Ovid and the Art of Love, and wrote the Bite of the Shoulder, of King Mark and Iseut the Blond, and the Metamorphosis of the Hoopoe and of the Swallow and of the Nightingale, now begins a new tale of a youth who was in Greece, of the lineage of King Arthur. . . ."

The foregoing list informs us that he wrote (1) a French version of Ovid's *Art of Love,* as I interpret the "Commands of Ovid and the Art of Love," contrary to the identification by some scholars of the "Commands" as the *Remedy of Love* (see *Ars Amatoria* II, 196); and (2) some of Ovid's *Metamorphoses.* None of the Ovidian translations have survived, except, perhaps, a story called "Philomena" included in the *Ovide moralisé* of the XIVth century, signed Chrestien li Gois. The ascription of this to Chrestien de Troyes is disputed. He also wrote what may have been the oldest version of the Tristan story, but it too is lost.

Of Chrestien's list, then, only the *Erec and Enid* and, of course, the *Cligés* have survived. After these, he wrote the *Knight of the Cart,* usually referred to by the name of the principal character as *Lancelot;* the *Knight of the Lion,* or *Yvain; William of England;* and last, *The Story of the Grail,* or *Perceval.* All of these later works have survived.

CHRESTIEN'S SOURCES

Because they have some bearing on the life of Chrestien, his statements concerning his sources are of special interest. Except for the lost translations from Ovid, we have none of the sources themselves, although he tells us where he supposedly obtained these tales. Again I quote his own statements:

Erec and Enid: "Chrestien de Troyes . . . derives from a story of adventure a pleasing argument about Erec the son of Lac, a story which those who earn a living by telling stories are accustomed to mutilate and spoil in the presence of kings and counts." It is to be noted that this is the only work in which he adds "de Troyes" to his baptismal name, which would seem to indicate that he was elsewhere when he wrote it.

Cligés: "This story which I wish to tell and relate to you, we find written in one of the books of the library of my lord Saint Peter at Beauvais. From it was extracted the tale of which Chrestien made this romance. The book is very old, which bears witness to the truth of the story, and for this it is more to be believed. By the books which we have we know the deeds of the ancients and of the world which once was."

Lancelot: "Since my lady of Champagne wishes me to undertake to write romances, I shall very gladly do so, as one who is entirely hers in whatever he can do in the world. . . . Chrestien begins his book of the *Knight of the Cart*. The Countess gives and hands over to him the material and the meaning, and he is concerned with thinking of putting scarcely anything in it except his effort and intention."

Yvain: "Chrestien ends his romance of the *Knight of the Lion*; nor did I ever hear more told of it, nor will you ever hear more, unless some one wishes to add a lie."

William of England: "Whoever would like to search out and inquire of the histories of England would find one which is worthy of belief, because it is pleasant and true, at Saint Esmoing [Bury St Edmunds] . . . . The material was told to me by a companion of mine, Roger the courtly . . . ."

Perceval: "Chrestien . . . who intends and strives to rhyme the best tale, by command of the Count [Philip of Flanders], that may be told in royal court: that is *The Story of the Grail*, of which the Count handed him the book . . . ."

To the above we can add two facts. First, Chrestien did not complete the *Lancelot*: "Godefroiz de Leigni, the cleric, has finished the *Cart*; but let no man blame him if he has worked upon Chrestien, for he has done this by the good will of Chrestien who began it: where Lancelot was immured, as far as the end of the story, so much has he done of it. . . ." Second, according to Gerbert de Montreuil, one of his continuators, Chrestien did not live to finish *The Story of the Grail*: "This, Chrestien de Troyes told us, who began of Perceval, but death which forestalled him did not let him bring it to an end."

Beyond what has been given, with the added possibilities of visits to Beauvais and England implied, there remains only to take a closer look at the two patrons named. The first of these, Marie (1145-1198), daughter of Louis VII of France and Eleanor of Aquitaine, was half-sister to Philip Augustus and to Richard the Lion Hearted. About 1159 she was married to Henry I, Count of Champagne from 1152 to 1181, who was a nephew of King Stephen of England and of Henry of Blois, Bishop of Winchester. Both Marie and Count Henry were patrons of literature, as shown by the numerous works dedicated to them.

The Story of the Grail is dedicated to, and was written at the behest of Philip of Alsace, born 1143, who became Count of Flanders in 1168, went on a Crusade in 1190, and died at Acre in 1191.

No clear explanation is available for the fact that only two of Chrestien's works are dedicated or, to be more accurate, written at the behest of named patrons. Scholars have inferred that this indicates that his early works were written at the court of Champagne, and that, for reasons unknown, he transferred his allegiance and person to the court of Flanders. This is not necessarily true, for the two families had many ties, too numerous and intricate to make clear here, including visits of Philip of Flanders to Champagne, relationships to the kings of England and France, and the marriage of Marie de Champagne, daughter of Henry I and Marie, to Baudouin IX, Count of Flanders and first Latin emperor of Constantinople.

Origins and Meaning of the Grail

Lacking both the book furnished Chrestien by Philip of Flanders and Chrestien's conclusion to his poem, scholars have sought an explanation of this work in many directions. Some have restricted themselves to Chrestien's poem; others have used one or the other of the many versions of the Grail story existing in various languages. The leading theories of the origin of the Grail story, briefly expressed, are the following:

1. The Byzantine theory, which finds equivalents for the elements of the Grail procession in the Byzantine Mass, and explains the Fisher King as Christ, the man in the inner room as the Holy Ghost.

2. The Ritual, or Vegetation theory, which would trace the origins to rites such as those of the Eleusinian mysteries.

3. The Celtic theory, according to which the Grail and attendant objects are the talismans of the Tuatha De Danann of ancient Celtic myth, the Grail perhaps a pagan cauldron of plenty.

4. The Judaeo-Christian theory, latest addition to the list, which finds the Grail an allegorical presentation of the conversion of the sacred relics of the Old Testament into the symbols of Christianity.

The presentations of these theories are varied, constituting an extensive body of scholarly writing. There are also other lesser theories.

CONTINUATIONS OF CHRESTIEN'S POEM

Manuscripts offer us a very lengthy body of Grail material in which other poets brought Chrestien's work to a conclusion. Following the 9,234 lines generally ascribed to him, the poem is extended over 11,000 more lines by an unknown poet, following which are some 12,000 lines by Wauchier de Denain, bringing the total to 33,755 lines. At this point we have two independent conclusions, one by Gerbert de Montreuil, of 17,000 lines, the other by Manessier, whose conclusion is 10,445 lines.

OTHER VERSIONS OF THE GRAIL STORY

Robert de Boron, between 1191 and 1201, is responsible for a 3,514-line poem, entitled the *Roman de l'estoire dou Graal* or *Joseph d'Arimathie*, which identifies the Grail as the Cup of the Last Supper and the Cup in which Christ's blood was collected at the Cross, and traces its transmission through the hands of Joseph of Arimathea and his relatives to England. It is this identification of the Grail with the Chalice that underlies most later Grail literature. Modern scholarship has applied this identification to Chrestien's Grail, leaving unsolved the lines in which Chrestien states that there is "neither pike nor lamprey nor salmon" in the Grail, which would seem to indicate that he had in mind a vessel for food. The mediaeval concept of a *"graal"* is best presented in the words of Hélinant de Froidmont: "a broad and not very deep bowl (*scutella lata et aliquantulum profunda*)." This concept also occurs in the Spanish Grail fragments, where the Grail is definitely a bowl (*escodilla*).

The *Didot-Perceval* presents a very interesting and compact Grail story in prose, which ties up the Grail adventure more closely with Merlin and the Arthurian court. Closely connected with Glastonbury, where the tomb of Arthur and Guenevere was supposedly discovered in 1191, is the *Perlesvaus*. In this the Grail Quest is undertaken by Gawain and then Lancelot. One of the finest of the Grail stories is the prose *Queste del Saint Graal*, the work of an unidentified Cistercian, who represents the Quest as a mystic search for the secrets of God, the search for ecstasy through grace. Its hero is the spotless son of Lancelot, Galaad, who appears here for the first time.

Greatest of the foreign versions is Wolfram von Eschenbach's *Parzifal*. Written between 1195 and 1210, it develops the theme of the Grail elaborately in some 25,000 lines. In it the Grail is a miraculous stone which sustains life through food and drink, and prevents death. The Grail castle is an important part of the total presentation, and introduces Lohengrin, son of Perceval. Especially intriguing is Wolfram's statement of his sources, as translated by Zeydel and Morgan:

> Kyot the bard known far and wide, 453-11
> Found in Toledo, cast aside,
> Set down in heathen writing,
> This story's source exciting . . . .
> A heathen, Flegetanis by name,
> In learning won the highest fame . . . .
> He wrote the Grail's adventures well . . . .

> Kyot, the master, dowed with wit, 455-2
> Was driven by this story
> To Latin volumes hoary . . .

> If master Cristjan, born at Troys, 827-1
> Impaired this tale with some alloy,
> Kyot then may justly rail,
> For he has told the authentic tale.

The Provençal, before he's done,
Relates . . .
From Provence into Germany
The story came, told properly,
Complete unto its very end.

No satisfactory explanation has been found for this ascription to Kyot the Provençal of a Grail story.

In the Welsh *Mabinogion*, the Grail castle scene in *Peredur* presents a lance from which three streams of blood fall, and the Grail is replaced by a large silver salver containing a man's head surrounded by blood. Peredur obtains the answers that Perceval did not: it is the head of his cousin, slain by the sorceresses of Gloucester, who had lamed his uncle. The sorceresses are slain. Here are no intimations of mystical qualities, no possible religious vessel.

Sir Perceval of Galles, a Middle English poem contained in the Thornton Romances, is a stanzaic life of Perceval generally paralleling Chrestien, with the striking omission of any reference to the Grail castle or the Grail.

Later Grail Treatments

Of the many appearances of the Grail in later literature, the one which has been most prominent in English is that in Sir Thomas Malory's *Le Morte d'Arthur*, based on French sources. Here, in Books XIII-XVII, the Sangreal, undescribed, appears at Arthur's court: "Then there entered into the hall the Holy Greal covered with white samite, but there was none might see it, nor who bare it. And there was all the hall fulfilled with good odours, and every knight had such meats and drinks as he best loved in this world." With Gawain the first to swear that he will seek the Grail, a hundred and fifty knights of the Round Table set out on a venture which is hopeless for most of them. At the Castle of Carbonek, the Grail appears to Galahad and Sir Bors and Sir Percivale: "Then looked they and saw a man come out of the holy vessel, that had all the signs of the passion of Jesu Crist . . . . Then took he himself the holy vessel and came to Galahad: 'This is,' said he, 'the holy dish wherein I ate the lamb on Sher-Thursday . . . . This night it shall depart from the kingdom of Logris [England] . . . .' " Galahad bears it to "the city of Sarras in the spiritual place." Percivale and Bors witness his death as king of this city, and "saw come from heaven an hand, but they saw not the body. And then it came right to the Vessel, and took it and the spear, and so bare it up to heaven. Sithen was there never man so hardy to say that he had seen the Sangreal."

In 1842, Alfred, Lord Tennyson published a volume of verse containing the poem "Sir Galahad," whom Tennyson described in the familiar lines:

> My good blade carves the casques of men,
> My tough lance thrusteth sure,
> My strength is as the strength of ten,
> Because my heart is pure.

In this poem the presentation of the Grail is:

> A gentle sound, an awful light!
> Three angels bear the Holy Grail;
> With folded feet, in stoles of white,
> On sleeping wings they sail.

In his *Idylls of the King* (1869), Tennyson has Percival, now a monk, tell the entire story of "The Holy Grail" to a fellow monk, Ambrosius. Percival and his fellow knights have sought "The cup, the cup itself, from which our Lord/Drank at the last sad supper with his own." After the cup had been brought to Glastonbury

by Joseph of Arimathea, it had healed people of their
ills, but the growth of evil in the land had caused it to
vanish. After the establishment of the Round Table,
the Grail is seen in a vision by a nun, Percival's sister:

> and then
> Streamed through my cell a cold and silver beam,
> And down the long beam stole the Holy Grail,
> Red-red with beatings in it as if alive . . . .

This vision is told to Percival, and he in turn repeats
to his brother knights the nun's injunction to fast and
pray. The Grail then appears in Arthur's hall:

> And in the blast there smote along the hall
> A beam of light seven times more clear than day;
> And down the long beam stole the Holy Grail
> All over cover'd with a luminous cloud,
> And none might see who bare it, and it past.

Of all those who leave in quest of a fuller vision, only
Lancelot, Bors, and Percival are allowed to come near
the Grail. Galahad alone achieves the perfect vision of
the blood-red Grail.

In the last part of the nineteenth century, Richard
Hovey, American poet, projected a long series entitled
Lancelot and Guenevere. A Poem in Dramas. Of the
nine dramas intended, only four were completed. The
last of these, *Taliesin,* foreshadows the fifth, which was
to have been *The Graal,* but, as it did Chrestien, death
forestalled Hovey. In *Taliesin,* Nimue, Lady of the
Lake, transfers Perceval in his sleep to the Grail castle.
Here King Evelac warns him not to be rash in seeking
the "Cup of Mystery, men call the Graal," that it is intended for Galahad. Perceval approaches the golden
doors of the sanctuary. The doors open, the splendor of
the Graal fills the place, but seven angels screen it from
his view. The angel Uriel, with a flaming sword, informs

Perceval that he is not yet pure enough to enter the holy place. The poetic quality of this preliminary scene makes the loss of Hovey's fifth play all the more regrettable.

The latest treatment of the Grail theme in English is to be found in T. S. Eliot's *The Waste Land*.

In the realm of music are two of the best known presentations of the Grail theme, *Parsifal* and *Lohengrin*, in which Richard Wagner combines the resources of poetic drama with those of music to give a modern treatment of the work of Wolfram von Eschenbach that is familiar to all opera lovers.

Thus the reader of today may look back, with a perspective of some eight hundred years, to Chrestien's *Story of the Grail* and marvel at the vitality of its great theme.

The Story of the Grail

Prologue

WHOEVER sows little, gathers little, and whoever wishes a fair harvest scatters his seed in such place that it returns fruit to him a hundred fold, for in land which is worth nothing good seed dries and fails. CRESTIENS makes a sowing of a romance that he begins, and sows it in so good a place that it cannot be without great worth, for he sows it for the most worthy man in the empire of Rome, Count PHELIPES, who is worth more than Alexander, who, they say, was so good. I shall prove that the Count is worth much more than he, for Alexander had amassed in himself all the vices and all the evils from which the Count is free and pure.

The Count is such that he does not listen to villainous boast or foolish word, and if he hears evil said of another, whoever it may be, it weighs upon him. The count loves right justice and loyalty and Holy Church and hates all villainy, and is more generous than one knows, for he gives, without hypocrisy and without guile, according to the Gospel, which says "Let not thy left hand know the good that thy right hand doeth." He knows it who receives it, and God, who sees all secrets and knows all the secret places in hearts and bowels.

Why does the GOSPEL say: "Conceal your good deeds from your left hand"? The left hand, according to the story, signifies the vain glory which comes from false hypocrisy. And the right hand, what does it signify?

Li Contes del Graal, lines 1-68.

Charity, which does not boast of its good work, but rather covers itself so that no one knows it except that one who is named God and charity. God is charity; and he who dwelleth in charity, according to the story (Saint Paul said it and I read it), dwelleth in God, and God in him. Therefore know well of truth that the gifts which the good Count Phelipes gives are of charity, for never does any-one advise him of them except his noble, debonair heart, which advises him to do good. Is he not worth more than Alexander was, who did not care for charity or for any good? Yes, never doubt it in any way. Then indeed will CRESTIENS have his labor safe, who intends and strives to rhyme the best tale, by the command of the Count, that may be told in royal court: that is THE STORY OF THE GRAIL, of which the Count handed him the book, and you shall hear how he succeeds in it.

The Son of the Widow

IT was in the time when trees flower, groves leaf, meadows turn green, and the birds in their latin sing sweetly in the morning, and everything flames with joy, that the son of the widow lady of the lonely Waste Forest got up, and it was no trouble for him to put his saddle on his hunter. He took three javelins, and thus sallied forth from his mother's manor at once. He thought that he would go see the harrowers who were harrowing his mother's oats. Twelve oxen and six harrows they had. Thus he entered the forest, and now the heart within him rejoiced on account of the soft weather and the song he heard of the birds which were making joy: all these things pleased him. Because of the serene weather, he took the bit from his hunter and let it go grazing over the fresh greening grass. And he, who knew well how to hurl them, went throwing his javelins around him, one backward and another forward, one low and another high, until he heard coming through the wood five knights in full armor. Their arms made very great noise, for often the branches of the oaks and of the hornbeams struck against them. The lances rattled against the shields and all the hauberks rustled. The wood rang; the iron of the shields and hauberks rang.

The youth hears and does not see those who are coming at more than a pace. He marvels at it and says:

Li Contes del Graal, lines 69-633.

"By my soul, my mother, my lady, told me true, who told me that devils are more noisy than anything in the world. And she said, to teach me, that because of them ought one to cross himself. But this instruction I shall disdain, for never indeed will I cross myself; rather will I strike the strongest so quickly with one of my javelins that never, as I believe, will any of the others approach me."

Thus spoke the youth to himself before he saw them; but when he saw them openly and they were no longer covered by the wood, and he saw the moving hauberks, the bright and shining helms, the lances and the shields, which he had never before seen, and saw the green and the vermilion gleam against the sun, and the gold and the azure and the argent, it pleased him fairly and nobly, and he said:

"Ah! Lord God, thanks! These are angels that I see here. Ah! truly have I sinned much, now have I acted very badly in saying that they were devils. My mother did not tell me a fable, who told me that angels were the most beautiful things there are, except God who is more beautiful than all. Here I see the Lord God, I believe, for I perceive one of them so beautiful that the others, if God keep me, haven't the tenth of beauty. My mother herself said that one is to believe and adore God and bow to Him and honor Him, so I shall adore this one and all the others with Him."

Straightway he throws himself to the ground and says all the creed and prayers that he knew, which his mother had taught him. The leader of the knights sees him and says:

"Stay back, for this youth who has seen us has fallen to earth for fear. If we all went together toward him, he would, it seems to me, have such great fear that he would die. Nor would he be able to answer anything that I might ask him."

They stop, and he passes on toward the youth at a great pace. He greets him and reassures him and says: "Youth, do not be afraid."

"I am not," says the youth, "by the Saviour in whom I believe. Are you God?"

"Not He, by faith."

"Who are you, then?"

"I am a knight."

"I never before knew a knight," says the youth, "nor did I see one nor ever hear one spoken of, but you are more beautiful than God. Would that I were now just as you, thus shining and thus made."

At this word the knight has drawn near him, and asks him: "Did you see five knights and three maidens in this plain today?"

The youth is intent on inquiring and asking other news: he reaches out his hand to his lance, grasps it and says: "Fair dear lord, you who are named knight, what is this you hold?"

"Now, it seems to me, have I succeeded very well," says the knight, "I thought, fair sweet friend, to learn news from you, and you wish to learn from me. I shall tell you: this is my lance."

"Do you say," says he, "that one throws it just as I do my javelins?"

"No indeed, youth, you are quite foolish. Rather does one strike with it on the spot.

"Then one of these three javelins is worth more; for I slay whatever I wish with it, birds and beasts at need, and I slay them from as far as one could draw a bolt."

"Youth, with this I have nothing to do, but answer me about the knights: tell me if you know where they are, and did you see the maidens?"

The youth grasps him by the corner of the shield and says: "What is this, and for what does it serve you?"

"Youth," says he, "this is trickery that you put me on other news than I request or ask of you. I thought, if God help me, that you would tell me news, rather than learn them of me, and you wish that I teach you. I shall tell to you, for I willingly agree with you. Shield is the name of what I am carrying."

"Shield is its name?"

"Truly," says he, "nor ought I to hold it vile, for it is of such good faith to me that, if anyone hurls or draws at me, it presents itself against all the blows: that is the service that it does me."

Meanwhile those who were behind came forward the full distance toward their lord and say to him quickly: "Lord, what said this Welshman to you?"

"He doesn't know all the laws," says the lord, "if God help me, for he never answers rightly anything I ask him. Rather he asks of whatever he sees, what is its name and what one does with it."

"Lord, know well that all Welshmen are by nature madder than beasts in pasture. This one is also like a beast. Mad is he who stops beside him, if he does not wish to muse and to waste his time in folly."

"I do not know," says he, "if God see me; before I set out on my way I shall tell him whatever he wishes. Never otherwise shall I depart from him."

Then he asks him again: "Youth," says he, "may it not grieve you, but tell me of the five knights and of the maidens likewise, if you encountered or saw them."

The youth held him caught by the skirt of the hauberk, and pulls it:

"Now tell me," says he, "fair lord. What is this that you have donned?"

"Youth," says he, "then you don't know it?"

"I, no."

"Youth, this is my hauberk, and it is as heavy as iron."

"Of iron, is it?"

"That you see well."

"Of this," says he, "I know nothing, but it is very beautiful, if God save me. What do you do with it and what is it worth to you?"

"Youth, that is easy to say: if you wanted now to hurl javelins or to loose an arrow at me, you would not be able to do me any harm."

"Lord knight, may God guard the does and stags with such hauberks, so that no one could slay any of them, nor might ever run after them."

The knight in turn says to him: "Youth, if the Lord God help you, if you know how, tell me news of the knights and maidens."

And he who was of little sense said to him: "Were you born thus?"

"No, youth, it can not be, for nothing can be born thus."

"Who then dressed you thus?"

"Youth, I shall indeed tell you who."

"Tell it then."

"Very gladly: it is not yet five entire days since all this harness was given me by King Arthur, who dubbed me. But now tell me: what became of those knights who came this way, who are escorting the three maidens? Are they going at a walk, or are they fleeing swiftly?"

And he says: "Lord, now look at that highest wood that you see which surrounds that mountain; those are the Straits of Valdone."

"What of that," says he, "fair brother?"

"My mother's harrowers are there, who are harrowing and plowing her lands; and if those people passed by there, if they saw them, they will tell it."

They tell him that they will go with him, if he leads them, to those who are harrowing the oats.

The youth takes his hunter and goes where the harrowers were harrowing the plowed lands where the oats are sown. When they saw their lord they all trembled with fright. Do you know why they did so? Because of the knights whom they saw, who came with him armed. For they well knew, if these had told him all their doing and their state, that he would like to be a knight, and his mother would go out of her senses. For they thought to hide him so that he might never see a knight or learn anything of their doing. The youth said to the oxherds:

"Did you see five knights and three maidens pass here?"

"They did not end today going through these straits," say the oxherds.

And the youth said to the knight who had talked to him so much:

"Lord, the knights and the maidens have passed this way. But now in turn tell me news of the King who makes knights and the place where he is most often found."

"Youth," says he, "I wish to tell you that the King sojourns at Carduel. The fifth day has not yet passed since he was sojourning there, for I was there and I saw him. If you do not find him, certainly there will be some one who will point him out to you: never will he be so hidden that you may not hear signs of him. But now I pray you that you teach me by what name I shall call you."

"Lord," says he, "I shall tell you: my name is 'Fair Son.'"

" 'Fair Son' is your name then? I believe that you have besides another name."

"Lord, by faith, my name is 'Fair Brother.' "

"Well do I believe you: but if you are willing to tell me the truth, I shall like to know your right name."

"Lord," says he, "I can indeed tell you that by my right name I am named 'Fair Lord.' "

"So help me God, that is a fair name. Have you any others?"

"Lord, not I, nor certainly did I ever have any others."

"So help me God, I hear marvels, the greatest that I ever heard, or, as I think, that I may ever hear."

At once the knight departs at a full gallop, for he is very anxious to overtake the others.

The youth did not hesitate to return to his manor, where his mother had her heart grieving and black because of his delay. Great joy she had when she saw him, nor was she able to conceal her joy, for, as a mother who loves much, she runs toward him and calls him "fair son, fair son," more than a hundred times:

"Fair son, much has my heart been distressed because of your staying. I have been so heart-rent by grief that I am almost dead. Where have you been so long today?"

"Where, lady? I shall tell you very well, never shall I lie about it, because I have had very great joy of a thing that I have seen. Then, did you not use to tell me that the angels of God our Lord are so very fair that never did Nature make such a beautiful creature, nor is there such a beautiful thing in the world?"

"Fair son, again do I say it indeed; I said it for true and say it again."

"Be quiet, mother! Did I not see just now the most beautiful things there are going through the Waste Forest? They are fairer, as I believe, than God or all His angels."

The mother takes him in her arms and says:

"Fair son, I render you unto God, for I have very great fear for you: you have seen, as I believe, the angels of whom people complain, who slay whatever they encounter."

"I have not, truly, mother, I have not, not! They say that they are named knights."

His mother faints when she hears him name a knight, and when she had straightened up again she spoke sadly:

"Ha! Alas! How badly I am treated! Fair sweet son, I thought to guard you so well from knighthood that you might never hear it spoken of, nor ever see anything of it. You should have been a knight, fair son, if it pleased God that he had protected your father and your other friends for you. There was no knight of such great worth, so dreaded nor so feared, fair son, as your father was, in all the Isles of the Sea. You can indeed boast that you fall away in nothing from his lineage nor mine, for I am born of knights, of the best of this country. In the Isles of the Sea there was no lineage better than mine in my age; but the best have fallen, and it is well known in many places that misfortunes happen to the worthy men who maintain themselves in great honor and in prowess. Baseness, shame, nor laziness does not fall, for it cannot; but the good must fall. Your father, and you do not know it, was wounded in the legs so that he remained a cripple. His great land, his great treasures, which he had as a worthy man, went entirely to ruin, and he fell into great poverty. The gentle men were wrongly impoverished, disinherited, and exiled after the death of Uterpendragon, who was king and father of the good King Arthur. The lands were devastated and the poor people outraged, so that he fled from there who was able to flee. Your father had this manor here in this Waste

Forest: he was not able to flee, but in great haste had himself brought in a litter, for elsewhere he did not know where he might hide. And you, who were small, had two very fair brothers. You were small, nursing, you were little more than two.

"When your two brothers were large, by the advice and counsel of their father, they went to two royal courts to obtain arms and horses. The eldest went to the king of Escavalon and served him until he was dubbed a knight; and the other, who was born afterward, went to King Ban of Gomeret. On one day both the youths were dubbed and made knights, and on one same day they moved to return to their abode, because they wished to give joy to me and their father, who afterward did not see them, for they were discomfited in arms. In arms they both died, for which I have great grief and great sorrow. Of the older there came marvels, for the ravens and crows picked out both his eyes; thus people found them dead. For grief of the sons, the father died, and I have suffered a very bitter life since he died. You were all my comfort and all my wealth; for there were no more of my people: nothing more had God left me of which I was joyous and glad."

The youth understands very little of what his mother is saying. "Give me," says he, "something to eat! I don't know of what you speak to me, but I should very willingly go to the King who makes knights. And I shall go, no matter whom it may worry."

The mother, as long as she can, holds him back and delays him. She prepares and makes ready for him a coarse shirt of canvas and drawers made in the fashion of Wales, where they make drawers and breeches together, it seems to me; and he had a coat and hood of deerskin closed around.

Thus the mother dressed him. Three days, no longer, she delayed him, for entreaty could do no more. Then the mother had strange grief, and kisses and hugs him weeping and says:

"Now have I very great grief, fair son, when I see you go away. You will go to the King's court, and will tell him to give you arms. There will be no contradiction, for he will give them to you, well do I know it; but when it comes to the test of bearing arms, how will it be then? How will you know how to succeed in doing what you never did nor saw another do? Badly, indeed, I fear: badly will you be trained in every way, nor is it any marvel, it seems to me, if one does not know what one has not learned. But a marvel it is when one does not learn what one hears and sees often.

"Fair son, I wish to teach you one sensible thing which you would do well to listen to and, if it please you, to retain; great good can come to you from it. You will be a knight very soon, son, if it please God, and I advise you, if you find either near or far any lady who has need of help, or disconsolate maiden, be ready to aid them, if they request it of you, for all honors depend on that. Whoever does not honor the ladies, his own honor must be dead. Serve ladies and maidens and you will be honored everywhere. If you entreat any one of them, take care that you do not annoy her. Do not do anything which may displease her. It is good to kiss a maiden, if she grants you the kiss. I forbid you the rest if you are willing to leave it for my sake. If she has a ring on her finger, or at her belt an alm's purse, if by love or by entreaty, she gives it to you, it will be good and fair to me that you carry away the ring: I give you leave to take the ring and the alm's purse.

"Fair son, I wish to tell you something else: Never,

on the way or in hostel, have a companion long without asking him his name; know the name of the person, for by the name one knows the man. Fair son, speak to worthy men, go with worthy men. A worthy man does not give bad counsel to those who keep his company. Above everything I wish to pray you that in church and in minster you go to pray Our Lord, that in this world He give you honor and give you so to conduct yourself in it that you may come to a good end."

"Mother," says he, "what is church?"

"A place where one does the service of Him who made heaven and earth and put men and beasts on it."

"And minsters what?"

"Son, this same: a beautiful and most holy house both of holy bodies and of treasures. One sacrifices there the Body of Jesus Christ, the holy prophet, to whom the Jews did many a shame. He was betrayed and judged wrongly, and suffered anguish of death for men and for women; for into hell souls used to go when they parted from the bodies, and He then cast them out of there. He was bound to the stake, beaten and then crucified, and wore a crown of thorns. To hear Masses and Matins and to adore that Lord, I advise you to go to the minster."

"Then I shall very willingly go to the churches and minsters," says the youth, "from now on; thus I make covenant of it with you."

Then there was no more delay. He takes his leave, and his mother weeps, and his saddle was already put on for him. In the manner and in the guise of Welshmen he was dressed: he had shod himself with rawhide shoes and everywhere that he went he was accustomed to carry three javelins. He wanted to carry his javelins along; but his mother had two of them taken away, because he resembled too much a Welshman. She would

have had all three taken very gladly, if it were possible.
In his right hand he carried a switch to strike his horse.
At the departure, weeping his mother kissed him, who
held him very dear and prays God that He have him.

"Fair son," says she, "may God give you much more
joy than remains to me, wherever you go!"

When the youth was distant the cast of a small stone,
he looked back and saw his mother fallen backward at
the head of the bridge. She lay in a faint as though she
had fallen dead. He struck his hunter across the crupper
with the switch and it went away. It did not stop, but
carried him away at a great pace, through the middle of
the great dark forest. He rode from early morning until
the day came to its decline. In the forest that night he
lay until the bright day appeared.

The Tent in the Meadow

IN the morning, to the song of the birds, the youth got up and mounted, and was intent on riding, until he saw a tent stretched in a beautiful meadow beside the source of a small spring. The tent was marvelously fair; one part was vermilion and the other green, banded with goldwork. Above, there was a golden eagle; the sun which was shining clear and vermilion was striking the eagle, and all the meadows gleamed from the illumination of the tent. In a circle around the tent, which was the most beautiful in the world, there were two leafy bowers and Welsh lodgings erected. The youth went toward the tent and said, before he reached it:

"God! now I see Your house. I should make a mistake if I did not go to adore You. Indeed my mother told me the truth when she told me that a minster was the most beautiful thing there is, and she told me that I should never find a church that I should not go in it to adore the Creator, in whom I believe. I shall go pray Him, by my faith, that He give me today to eat, for I have great need of it."

Then he comes to the tent, and finds it open, and amid the tent a bed covered with a cover of striped silk. He sees in the bed a damsel lying all alone sleeping. Her company was far, her maidens had gone to gather new flowrets to strew through the tent as they were wont to do. When the youth entered the tent, his horse stumbled

Li Contes del Graal, lines 634-832.

so heavily that the damsel heard it, and awakened and started. The youth, who was silly, said: "Maiden, I greet you, as my mother taught me; my mother taught me and said that I should greet the maidens in whatever place I might find them."

The maiden trembles from fear on account of the youth, who seems to her mad, and thinks herself a proven fool because he has found her alone. "Youth," says she, "keep your way! Flee, so that my friend may not see you!"

"Rather will I kiss you, by my head," says the youth, "whomever it may grieve; as my mother taught me."

"I, truly, will never kiss you," says the maiden, "if I can help it. Flee, so that my friend may not find you; because, if he finds you, you are dead."

The youth had strong arms and he embraces her very sillily, for he did not know how to do otherwise: he put her beneath him at full length and she defended herself greatly and avoided all that she could, but defense was of no avail, for the youth rapidly kissed her, whether she were willing or not, twenty times, as the tale says, until he saw on her finger a ring with a very bright emerald. "Further," said he, "my mother told me that I should take the ring from your finger, but that I should do nothing more to you. Here now, the ring, I wish to have it!"

"My ring you shall never have, truly," says the maiden, "know it well, if you do not snatch it from my finger by force."

The youth takes her by the hand; by force he stretches her finger. He took the ring from her finger and put it on his own and said: "Maiden, may all be well with you, now I shall go away well paid. It is much better to kiss you than any chambermaid there is in all my mother's house, for you do not have a bitter mouth."

She weeps and says to the youth: "Do not carry away my ringlet, for I should be mistreated for it, and you would lose your life for it, however delayed it may be, I promise you."

The youth does not take to heart anything of what he hears, but because he had fasted he was dying of hunger in evil manner. He finds a keg full of wine and a cup of silver beside it, and sees on a chest of reed a new white cloth. He lifts it up and beneath finds three good pastries of fresh mutton. This food did not annoy him; on account of the hunger which has him in great anguish, he crushes one of the pastries before him and eats with great zest and pours some of the wine into the silver cup, which was not a bit ugly. He drinks often and in great gulps and says: "Maiden, these pastries will not be wasted by me today. Come eat, they are very good; each will have enough of his own, and there will remain one of them entire." She weeps during this time, however much he begs and entreats her, and does not answer a word, but sobs tenderly and strong. Very harshly does she wring her hands. He ate as much as pleased him and drank until he had enough and covered the remainder again.

Then he took leave straightway and commended to God, her to whom his greetings were not pleasing.

"God save you," says he, "fair friend! But for God's sake may it not worry you about your ring that I now carry away, for before I die of death I shall recompense you for it; I am departing, with your leave."

She weeps and says that never will she commend him to God; for it will befall her because of him to have so much shame and so much trouble that never did any miserable woman have as much, nor will she ever have help or aid from him as long as he may live; and let him know well that he has betrayed her.

Thus she remained weeping. Then there was scarcely any delay before her friend returned from the wood: he saw the tracks of the youth, who went on his way, and it grieved him, and he found his friend weeping, and said: "Damsel, I believe by these signs I see that there has been a knight here."

"There has not, lord, I assure you of it, but there was a Welsh youth here, annoying and villainous and stupid, who has drunk of your wine as much as pleased him and seemed good to him, and he ate of your three pastries."

"And for this, fair one, you weep so? If he had drunk and eaten everything, I should have been willing."

"There is more to it, lord," says she, "my ring is in the quarrel; for he has taken it from me, and carries it away: I should rather be dead than that he should have thus carried it away."

Behold him discomforted and in anguish in his heart. "By my faith," says he, "here is an outrage! And since he carries it away, let him have it; but I think that he did more: if there was more, don't conceal it."

"Lord," says she, "he kissed me."

"He kissed you?"

"Indeed, I certainly told you so; but it was against my will."

"Rather it sat well with you and pleased you. Never was there any opposition," says he, whom jealousy anguishes, "do you believe that I don't know you? I do, certainly, I know you well, nor am I so cross-eyed or so one-eyed that I do not see your falsity. You have entered into an evil path. You have entered into evil pain, for never will your horse eat oats, nor be bedded down until I am avenged for it, and there where he throws a shoe, never more will he be shod again. If he dies, you will follow me on foot, and never more will the clothes in which you are dressed be changed. Rather will you follow me on foot and naked until I have taken his head; never shall I do other justice."

At once he sat down and ate.

The Vermilion Knight

THE youth rode until he saw a charcoal burner coming, driving before him an ass.

"Villein," says he, "you who are driving the ass before you, teach me the straightest way to Carduel. King Arthur, whom I wish to see, makes knights there, so they say."

"Youth," says he, "in this direction there is a castle seated above the sea. You will find King Arthur, fair sweet friend, glad and grieving at that castle, if you go there."

"Now will you tell me, according to my wish, of what the King has joy and grief?"

"I shall tell you," says he, "very quickly: King Arthur with all his host has fought against King Rion. The King of the Isles was conquered; and of this is King Arthur glad, and angry at his companions who departed to the castles, where they saw the best abode, nor does he know how it goes with them; of this is the grief that the King has."

The youth does not prize worth a penny the news of the charcoal burner, except that he entered into the way, in the direction that he showed him, until he saw by the sea a very well placed and strong and fair castle, and sees come forth through the gate an armed knight, who carried a gold cup in his hand. He held his lance and rein and shield in his left hand, and the gold cup in his right hand; and his arms, which were all vermilion, fitted him well.

Li Contes del Graal, lines 833-1304.

The youth saw the beautiful arms, which were fresh and new; they pleased him and he said:

"By faith, I shall ask the King for those: if he gives them to me, fair will it be to me, and cursed be he who wishes others!"

Then he ran toward the castle, for he was anxious to come to court, until he came near to the knight, and the knight detained him a little, and asked him: "Where will you go, youth? Tell me!"

"I wish," says he, "to go to court to ask those arms of the King."

"Youth," says he, "you will do well. Now go quickly and come back, and this much will you say to the sorry King: if he does not wish to hold his land of me, let him yield it up to me, or let him send someone to defend it against me, for I say that it is mine. And believe, by these tokens, that I took from in front of him just now, together with the wine he was drinking, this cup that I am carrying away."

Now let him seek someone else who may repeat it, for this one has not understood a word of it. He did not stop until he reached the court where the King and his knights were seated at their meal. The hall was level with the ground, and the youth entered on horseback into the hall, which was paved and as long as wide. King Arthur was seated pensively at the head of a table, and all the knights were talking; the ones were amusing the others, except him who was pensive and silent. The youth came forward, and he did not know which one he should greet, for he recognized nothing of the King, until Yonez, who held a knife in his hand, came to meet him.

"Youth," says he, "you who come there, who hold the knife in your hand, show me which one is the King."

Yonez, who was very courteous, said to him: "Friend, there he is!"

At once he went toward him and greeted him as best he knew how. The King was thinking and did not say a word. He addressed him another time; the King thought and did not sound a word.

"By my faith," said the youth then, "this King never made a knight. When one cannot draw a word out of him, how could he make a knight?"

At once he makes ready to turn away. He turns the head of his hunter, but in the guise of a man of little sense he had led him so close to the King, that, without any fable, he knocked a bonnet cap off his head and onto the table before him. The King turned toward the youth his head, which he was holding lowered, and wholly left his thought and said:

"Fair brother, welcome! I pray you that you hold it not ill that I was silent at your greeting. I could not answer you for anger, for the worst enemy I have, who hates me most, has here gainsaid me my land, and he is such a fool that he says he will have it free of claim, whether I am willing or not. He is named the Vermilion Knight of the Forest of Quinqueroi. And the Queen had come to sit here before me to see and comfort these knights who are wounded. The knight would hardly have angered me by anything he said, but he took my cup from in front of me and lifted it so foolishly that he poured all the wine with which it was filled on the Queen. This was ugly and villainous work, for the Queen, inflamed with great grief and anger because of it, has entered her room, where she is killing herself, nor do I think, so help me God, that she can ever escape alive."

The youth does not prize worth a chive whatever the King says and relates to him, nor does he care about the Queen's grief or shame.

"Make me a knight, lord King," says he, "for I wish to go away."

Clear and laughing were the eyes in the head of the wild youth. No one who sees him considers him wise, but all those who saw him held him for handsome and gentle.

"Friend," says the King, "get down and hand over your hunter to that youth. He will take care of it and will do your will. It will be done, I vow it to Lord God, to my honor and to your gain."

The youth answered: "Never were those whom I met on the plain dismounted, and you wish that I dismount? Never, by my head, shall I dismount; but do it quickly, and I shall depart."

"Ha!" says the King, "fair dear friend, I shall do it very willingly, to your gain and to my honor."

"Faith that I owe the Creator," says the youth, "fair lord King, I shall not be a knight for months if I am not a vermilion knight. Give me the arms of that one whom I met outside the door, who is carrying off your golden cup."

The seneschal, who was wounded, was angered by what he heard and said: "Friend, you are right; go take the arms from him straightway, for they are yours. You did not act a bit foolishly when you came here for that."

"Keu," says the King, "for God's mercy! Too willingly you say annoying things, and you never care to whom. In a worthy man, that is too ugly a vice because, if the youth is silly, yet he is, I hope, a very gentle man. If it comes to him from teaching because he has been to a villainous teacher, he can yet be worthy and wise. It is evil to mock another and to promise without giving. A worthy man ought not to undertake to promise anything to another that he cannot or will not give him, lest he gather the ill will of him who, without the promise, is his friend and, as soon as it has been promised to him, gapes to have the promise. By this can you know that it would be better to deny a man than make him gape; and if anyone would like to tell the truth of it, he mocks and deceives himself who makes a promise and does not pay it, for he takes from himself the heart of his friend." Thus the King spoke to Keu.

The youth, who was leaving, saw a fair and gentle maiden, and greeted her and she him and smiled at him, and in smiling said to him this much: "Youth, if you live to grow old enough, I think and believe in my heart that in all the world there will not be nor will anyone know in it any better knight than you: thus do I think and consider and believe." The maiden had not smiled for more than the past six years, and she said this so loudly that all heard it.

Keu, whom the words annoyed much, leaped up, and gave her such a stout blow with his palm on her tender face that he caused her to stretch out on the floor. When he had struck the maiden, on his return he found a fool standing beside a fireplace and thrust him into the burning fire with his foot through wrath and ire because the fool was wont to say: "This maiden will not smile until she shall see the one who will have all the lordship of knighthood." Thus he cries, and she weeps.

The youth does not stay, but turns away without counsel after the Vermilion Knight. Yonez, who knew all the straight paths and very willingly brought news to court, all alone, without companions, goes down through a garden beside the hall and by a postern gate until he came to the quite straight road, where the knight was awaiting knighthood and adventure. The youth at a great pace came toward him to take his arms, and the knight in order to wait had put the golden cup down on a large block of dark stone. When the youth had approached him until the one could hear the other, he cried out to him:

"Put down those arms; do not carry them any more, for King Arthur so orders you."

The knight asks him: "Youth, does no one dare come here to maintain the right of the King? If anyone is coming, do not conceal it."

"What, devil, is this now a boast, lord knight, that you make to me, that you have not yet drawn off my arms? Take them off quickly, I command you!"

"Youth," says he, "I ask you if anyone is coming here, on behalf of the King, who wishes to fight with me."

"Dan knight, now take the arms off quickly, lest I take them off you, for I would not suffer you to have them any longer. Know well that I would strike you if you made me talk about them any more."

Then the knight was angered, he raised his lance with both hands, and gave him such a neckblow with it across the shoulders with the wooden shaft that he knocked him down on the neck of his horse. The youth became angered when he felt that he was wounded by the neckblow that he had taken. As best he can he aims at his eye and lets go a javelin; so that he does not listen or see or hear it, he strikes him amid the eye and brain so that on the other side on the nape of his neck he spreads his blood and his brain. His heart fails from the pain and he bends back and falls at full length.

The youth dismounts and puts the lance to one side and separates the shield from his neck, but he does not know how to succeed with the helmet on his head, for he does not know how he may take it, and he has a desire to unsheath his sword, but doesn't know how to do it, nor can he draw it from the scabbard, but seizes the scabbard and jerks and pulls. Yonez begins to laugh when he sees the youth in difficulty. "What is this, friend?" says he. "What are you doing?"

"I don't know what: I believed of your King that he had given me these arms, but I shall sooner have wholly chopped the dead man to pieces than carry away any of his arms, for they hold so to the body that that within and this outside are all one, as it seems to me, they hold together so."

"Now don't be dismayed in any way; for I shall very well separate them, if you wish," says Yonez.

"Do it quickly then," says the youth, "and give them to me without delay." At once Yonez divests him and takes off his breeches as far as his big toe. There remained neither hauberk nor other armor; but the youth did not wish to leave his own clothing, nor would he take, for anything that Yonez said to him, a very comfortable tunic of cloth of quilted silk that the knight wore beneath his hauberk when he was alive, nor could Yonez take off his feet the rawhide shoes with which he was shod. Rather he said: "The devil! Is this now a joke that I should change my good clothes, that my mother made for me the other day, for the clothes of this knight? My coarse great shirt of canvas for this one which is soft and thin? Would you wish that I leave my little tunic that water does not pass through for this one which would not hold a drop? Shamed be his whole throat who will change either far or near his good clothes for another's bad ones!"

It's a very heavy thing to teach a fool: he would not take anything except the arms, for any prayer that is made to him. Yonez laces the breeches for him and over the rawhide shoes puts on him the spurs on top of the hose. Then he dressed him in the hauberk so that never was anyone better, and on the coif he sets the helmet, which fits him very well; and of the sword he teaches him that he gird it on loose and hanging. Then he puts

his foot in the stirrup and makes him mount on the
charger.   Never before had he seen a stirrup nor did
he know anything of a spur, only of whip or switch.
Yonez brings him the shield and the lance, then hands
them to him. Before Yonez goes away, the youth says:
"Friend, take my hunter and lead him away; for he is
very good, and I give him to you, because I have no more
need of him.   Carry his cup to the King and greet him
on my behalf; and this much you will say to the maiden
whom Keu struck on the jaw, that, if I can, before I die,
I think to put him to cook so well that she will hold herself avenged."

He answers that he will deliver his cup to the King,
and will accomplish his message according to the law of
the Preacher.

At once they part, and go away.   Yonez, bringing
the cup back to the King, enters through the middle of the
door into the hall where the barons are and says:

"Sire, now rejoice, for your knight who was here
sends your cup back to you."

"Of what knight are you speaking?" asks the King,
who was still in his great wrath.

"In the name of God, sire," says Yonez, "I speak
of the youth who just now departed from here."

"Are you speaking of the Welshman," says the
King, "who asked me for the sinople-tinted arms of the
knight who has done me many a shame according to his
power?"

"Sire, I am in truth speaking of him."

"How did he have my cup?   Does that one like him
and prize him so much that he gave it over to him of his
own will?"

"Rather the youth sold it to him so dearly that he
killed him."

"How was that, fair friend?"

"Sire, I do not know, except that I saw that the knight struck him with his lance and did him great annoyance, and the youth struck him in turn in the middle of the eye with a javelin so that he made his blood and brains spread out behind him, and stretched him upon the ground dead."

Then said the King to the seneschal: "Ha! Keu, how you have done me harm today by your envious tongue, which has said many a foolish thing. You have taken from me a knight who this day has been worth much to me."

"Sire," says Yonez to the King, "by my head, he sends word by me to the Queen's maiden, whom Keu struck in provocation through ill will and in despite of him, that he will avenge her, if he lives, and if he can have the chance."

The fool, who was sitting beside the fire, hears the word and leaps to his feet and comes before the King all glad and has such joy that he stamps and jumps and says:

"Dan King, if God save me, now your adventures approach. Felonious and harsh ones will you see happen often, and I can covenant with you that Keu can be quite certain that in an ill hour saw he his feet and hands and his foolish and villainous tongue, for, before forty days have passed, the knight will have avenged the kick that he gave me, and the slap that he gave the maiden will be very dearly sold and well paid for and returned, for he will break his right arm for him between the elbow and the armpit. A half year he will carry it hanging from his neck, and well may he carry it there; he cannot escape it any more than death."

This word grieved Keu so much that he almost burst from ill will and wrath, and indeed he almost went to thrash him before all. He might have killed him, but because it might displease the King, he left off and did not attack him. And the King said:

"Hai! Hai! Keu, how you have angered me today! If any one had directed and guided the youth with the arms until he knew how to help himself a little with them, both with the shield and the lance, he would be a good knight without doubt. But he knows neither little nor much of arms, nor of anything else. He would not even know how to draw the sword, if he needed it.

"Now he sits armed on his horse, and he will meet some vassal who will not be afraid to cripple him to gain his horse. He will have quickly killed or crippled him, for he will not know how to defend himself, he is so silly and like the dumb beasts, he will quickly have made his attack."

Thus the King laments and regrets the youth and shows a sad face, but he can not gain anything by it, so he lets the talk stand.

Gornemant de Goort

THE youth went spurring through the forest without stopping until he came to the level lands by a river, which was more than a crossbow shot in width, and all the water had again entered and withdrawn into its proper conduit. Toward the great river, which is noisy, he went across a wide meadow, but he did not enter into the water, for he saw it very deep and black and much swifter than the Loire; so he went along the shore beside a great smooth cliff, which was on the other side of the water so that the water beat at its feet.

On that rock, on a slope which descended toward the sea, there was a rich and strong castle. Where the water flowed toward the bay, the youth turned to the left and saw the towers of the castle born, for it seemed to him that they were nascent, and that they were coming forth from the castle. In the middle of the castle there was standing a tower both strong and great; it had a very strong barbican, which opposed the sea, turned toward the bay, and the sea beat at its feet. At the four sides of the wall, which was of squared hard stone blocks, there were four low turrets which were very strong and beautiful. The castle was very well placed and quite comfortable within. In front of the round castlet there was a bridge built over the water, of stone and copper and lime. The bridge was both strong and high, battlemented all around; for amid the bridge there was a tower and in

Li Contes del Graal, lines 1305-1698.

front a drawbridge which was made and established as it should rightly be: by day a bridge, at night a door. The youth makes his way toward the bridge. Dressed in a robe of ermine, a worthy man was going along entertaining himself on the bridge and awaits him who was coming toward the bridge. The worthy man was holding in his hand a small staff for support, and behind him came two youths, completely uncloaked. He who comes has well retained what his mother taught him, for he greeted him and said: "Lord, this my mother taught me."

"God bless you, fair brother!" says the worthy man, who recognized and knew him as silly and foolish by his speech, and asked: "Fair brother, whence come you?"

"Whence? From the court of King Arthur."

"What did you do there?"

"The King, may he have good fortune, has made me a knight."

"Knight? If God give me well-being, I did not think that at this point he would remember such a thing. I thought that he had other things to do than to make knights. Now tell me, debonair brother, who gave you those arms?"

"The King," says he, "gave them to me."

"Gave? How?"

He tells him as you have heard the tale; if it were told another time, it would be annoying and idle talk, for no story is improved by that. The worthy man asks him further what he knows how to do with his horse.

"I run him uphill and down just as I used to run the hunter when I had taken him at my mother's house."

"Tell me further of your arms, fair friend: what do you know how to do with them?"

"I know well how to don them and take them off just as the youth armed me with them, who in front of me disarmed of them him whom I had killed; and I wear them so lightly that they do not grieve me in anything."

"By the soul of God, this prize I well," says the worthy man, "and well does it suit me. Now tell me, if it doesn't annoy you, what need brought you here."

"Lord, my mother taught me that I should go toward worthy men and that I should take counsel with them and I should believe what they would say, for worth have those who believe them."

The worthy man answers: "Fair brother, blessed be your mother that she advised you so well! But do you wish to say something else?"

"Yes."

"What?"

"So much and no more, than that you lodge me today."

"Very willingly," says the worthy man, "provided that you grant me a gift whence you will see great good come."

"And what?" says he.

"That you believe the counsel of your mother and me."

"By my faith," says he, "I grant it."

"Then dismount." And he dismounts.

One of the two youths who had come there takes his horse, and the other disarmed him, so that he remained in the foolish dress, in the rawhide shoes and in the badly made and badly cut tunic of deerskin which his mother had given him. The worthy man had the cutting spurs of sharp steel, which the youth had brought, put on his heels, and he mounts the horse and hangs the shield from his neck by the cord and takes the lance and says:

"Friend, now learn of arms and take heed how one should hold lance, and spur on or hold back a horse." Then he displayed the ensign, and instructs and teaches him how he ought to take his shield; he makes it hang a little forward so that he joins it to the neck of the horse, and puts the lance on the felt, and spurs the horse, which was worth a hundred marks, for none went more willingly, more quickly, nor with greater vigor. The worthy man knew much of the shield, the horse, and the lance, for he had learned it from his youth. Everything that the worthy man did pleased and suited the youth. When he had made his provocation well and fair before the youth, who had paid close heed to it, he comes back, lance raised, to the youth and asks him:

"Friend, would you also know how to handle the lance and the shield and to spur and guide the horse?"

And he said freely that he would be willing not to live another day nor have land nor wealth provided he might know how to do the same.

"That which one does not know, one can learn," says the worthy man, "fair dear friend, if he wishes to take pains and to understand. It behooves in all trades to have pains and heart and practice. By these three one can know everything. If you never did it nor saw another do it, if you do not know how to do it, you have no shame or blame for it."

Then the worthy man made him mount, and he began to carry lance and shield as adroitly as though he had lived all his days in tournaments and in wars and gone through all the lands seeking battle and adventure; for it came to him from nature, and when nature teaches it and the heart is all intent on it, it cannot be a painful thing in which nature and heart take pains. By these two he did so well that it pleased the worthy man much, and he said in his heart that if he had taken pains and busied himself all his life he would have been very well taught in it. When the youth had made his turn before the worthy man, on his return, lance raised, he repairs to him, just as he had seen him do, and said:

"Lord, have I done it well? Do you believe indeed I need to take pains, if I wish to take pains in this? Never did my eyes see anything of which I had so great a desire; much would I wish that I might know as much as you know of it."

"Friend, if you have your heart in it," says the worthy man, "much will you know of it, indeed in an ill hour will you have any worry."

The worthy man three times mounted, three times taught him of arms all that he knew how to show him until he had shown him enough of it, and three times made him mount. At the last he said to him:

"Friend, if you met a knight, what would you do if he struck you?"

"I should strike him back."

"And if your lance shattered?"

"After that there would be nothing more to do except that I should run upon him with my fists."

"Friend, that you would not do."

"What shall I do then?"

"You will go to seek him with sword play."

Then the worthy man, who much desires to teach and instruct him in arms so that he may know well how to defend himself with the sword, if anyone seek him out, or to attack when there is place for it, fixes his lance before him in the ground so it stood straight, then he put the sword in his hand.

"Friend," says he, "in this manner you will defend yourself, if anyone attacks you."

"Of this," says he, "if God save me, no one knows as much as I do, for with the horse collars and bucklers at my mother's home I have learned much of it, until I was often wearied by it."

"Then let us go today to the hostel," says the worthy man, "for there is nothing else, and you will have, whomever it may annoy, hostel tonight without villainy."

Then they go off side by side and the youth said to his host: "Lord, my mother taught me that I should never go with a man nor should I have any company with him greatly, unless I knew his name; and if she taught me wisely, I wish to know your name."

"Fair sweet friend," says the worthy man, "my name is Gornemant de Goort."

Thus they come to the hostel, hand in hand both chat together. At the mounting of a step came a youth wholly of his own will who brought a short mantle. He runs to cloak the youth with it, so that after the heat, cold should not seize him which would do him harm. The worthy man had rich lodgings, beautiful and large, and fine servants; and the food was made ready, good and fair and well prepared; so the knights washed, then sat down to eat. The worthy man seated the youth beside him and had him eat with him from one bowl. I give no other news of the foods, how many of them there were nor what they were, but they ate and drank enough; I make no other account of the meal.

When they had gotten up from the table the worthy man, who was very courteous, prayed the youth who sat beside him to remain a month; he would gladly keep him a full year, if he were willing, and he might learn meanwhile such things, if they pleased him, that in need would be of use to him. And the youth said afterward:

"Lord, I do not know whether I am near to the

manor where my mother dwells, but I pray God that He lead me to her, and that I may be able to see her again; for I saw her fall in a faint at the head of the bridge before her door, and I do not know if she is alive or dead. When I left her she fell in a faint from grief for me, well do I know it, and because of that, I could not, until I knew her condition, make a long sojourn, rather shall I go way tomorrow at dawn."

The worthy man heard that prayer availed nothing, and the talk fails; so they go to bed without more pleading, for the beds were already made.

The worthy man arose early in the morning and went to the bed of the youth where he found him lying, and he had carried to him as a present shirt and drawers of white cloth and breeches dyed in brazil and tunic of a cloth of India silk which was woven and made in India; in order that he might have him dress he sent them to him and said to him: "Friend, you will put on these clothes that you see here, if you believe me."

The youth answers: "Fair lord, you could say much better; are not the clothes that my mother made me then worth more than these, and you wish that I put these on?"

"Youth, by the faith I owe my head," says the worthy man, "rather are they worth less. You told me, fair friend, when I brought you in here, that you would do all my commands."

"And so shall I do," says the youth, "never shall I be against you in anything."

He does not delay any longer in putting on the clothes, so has he left those his mother gave him. The worthy man stooped down and put on his foot his right spur: the custom used to be such that he who made a knight was to put on his spur for him. There were many other youths, of whom each who could come there put

his hand to arming him. The worthy man took the
sword and girded it on him and kissed him and said that
he has given him with the sword the highest order that
God has made and commanded, that is the order of
knighthood, which should be without villainy, and said:

"Fair brother, now remember: if it happens that it behoove you to fight against any knight, this I wish to
say and pray you: if you overcome him so that he can
no longer defend himself against you or oppose you, but
rather must call for mercy, that you do not knowingly
slay him. And take care that you be not too talkative or
too much a teller of tales. No one can be too talkative
without often saying such things that may be thought
villainous of him, and the Preacher says and relates:
'Who talks too much, does a sin.'

"For this, fair brother, I warn you of too much speaking. And I also pray you: if you find man or woman,
whether she be damsel or lady, disconsolate for any thing,
counsel them, so will you do well, if you know how to
counsel them and if you have the power.

"One other thing I teach you, and do not consider it
with disdain, for it is not at all to be disdained: go willingly to the minster to pray to Him who made everything, that He have mercy on your soul and that in this
earthly world He protect you as His Christian."

And the youth said to the worthy man: "By all the
apostles of Rome may you be blessed, fair lord, for I
heard my mother say the same."

"Now don't ever again say, fair brother," says the
worthy man, "that your mother taught and instructed
you. I do not blame you if you have said it up to now,
but from now on, by your mercy, I pray you that you
take heed. If you said it any more, people would hold it
for folly, for this I pray you beware of it."

"What shall I say then, fair lord?"

"The vavassor, this can you say, who put on your spur for you, instructed and taught it to you."

And he has given the worthy man the gift that as long as he shall live never more will there be sounded a word except of him; for it seems to him that this is good which he teaches him. The worthy man now makes the sign of the Cross over him, and raised his hand high and said:

"Fair lord, God save you! Go with God, and may He guide you; for I see the delay annoys you."

Blancheflor and Belrepeire

THE new knight departs from his host, and he is very anxious to come to his mother and find her healthy and alive, so he puts himself into the lonely forests, for he knew his way in the forests much better than on plain lands, and rides until he sees a strong and well placed castle; but outside the walls there was nothing except sea and water and waste land. He hastens to travel toward the castle until he arrives in front of the gate, but before he comes to the gate he has to pass a bridge so weak that he believes it will hardly hold him up. The knight mounts upon the bridge and passed it without ill or shame or encumbrance happening to him. He came in front of the gate and found it closed and locked, nor did he knock on it softly nor did he call in a low voice; he struck so much that quickly a lean and pale maiden came to the windows of the hall and said: "Who is it who calls there?"

He looks toward the maiden, sees her and says: "Fair friend, I am a knight who prays you that you let me enter and lend me hostel this night."

"Lord," says she, "you shall have it, but you will never be grateful to us for it; nevertheless, we shall provide you with as good hostel as we are able."

Then the maiden drew back and he who keeps watch at the gate fears that they may make him stand too long, so he begins to knock again. At once four sergeants

Li Contes del Graal, lines 1699-2971.

came who held great axes on their shoulders and each
one had girded on a sword. They have opened the gate
and say: "Lord, come in!"

If all had been well with the sergeants, they might
have been handsome, but they had had so much ill
fortune, they were such from fasting and keeping vigil,
that one might marvel at them. And if he had indeed
found the land outside waste and bare, inside nothing
made it better for him, for everywhere he went he found
the streets desolate and the old houses fallen in, for
there was in them neither man nor woman. There were
two minsters in the town which were two abbeys, the
one of trembling nuns, the other of dejected monks. He
did not find the minsters well adorned nor well tapestried;
rather he saw the walls cracked and split and the towers
uncovered, and the houses were open night and day. No
mill grinds there, nor oven bakes in any place in the
whole castle; nor was there bread nor cake nor anything
which might be sold by which one might gain a denier.

Thus he found the castle. For there was in it neither
bread nor pastry, nor wine nor cider nor beer. Toward
a palace covered with slate the four sergeants have led
him and dismounted and disarmed him. At once a youth
comes down the steps of the hall bringing a gray mantle.
He put it around the knight's neck, and another stabled
his horse where there was no wheat nor hay nor fodder
except a little, for there was none in the house. The
others have him go up the steps in front of them. In
the hall, which was very beautiful, two worthy men and
a maiden came to meet him. The worthy men were white-
haired, not so much that they were completely white.
They would have been of fine age with all their strength
and all their force if they did not have trouble and
worry. And the maiden came, more elegant and more

adorned and more svelte than sparrow hawk or parrot.
Her mantle and her bliaut were of a dark purple, starred
with miniver, and the lining was not hairless, but of
ermine; the mantle was edged at the neck with a black
and white zibeline which was not too long nor too wide.
And if I ever made a description of beauty that God
had put in body of woman or in face, now it pleases me
to make another in which I shall not lie by a word. She
was unveiled and had hair such, if it could be, that anyone who saw it would indeed think it was all of fine
gold, it was so shining and golden. Her forehead was
white and high and smooth as though it were worked
by hand of man, of stone or ivory or of wood; brown
eyebrows and wide spacing between her eyes; in her head
her eyes were laughing and gray, clear and wide. Her
nose was straight and extended, and the vermilion seated
on the white fitted better on her face than sinople on
argent. To steal sense and heart of people God made
of her a passing marvel, never after did He make her equal
nor had He before her. When the knight sees her, he
greets her and she and both the knights greet him; and
the damsel takes him by the hand debonairly and said:

"Fair lord, our hostel, certainly, will not be such
tonight as would be fitting for a worthy man. If I
told you right now our condition and our state you
would believe, perhaps, that I was saying it through malice
in order to make you go away, but, if you please, now
come, take the hostel such as it is, and God give you
better tomorrow."

Thus she leads him by the hand into a ceiled room
which was very beautiful and long and wide. On a
quilt of samite which was spread on a bed they both sat
down. Therein knights four, five, and six came in and sat
down all in groups and said not a word, and they saw

him sitting beside their lady and not saying a word. He
held himself from speaking because he remembered the
warning that the worthy man had given him. All the
knights in council held great discussion of him with one
another.

'God!" says each one, "I marvel much if this
knight is mute. It would be great grief; for never
so fair a knight was born of woman: he is very be-
fitting beside my lady, and my lady also beside him,
if they were not both mute. He is so handsome and she
so beautiful that never did knight and maiden come together so well; it seems that God made one for the other
so that He might put them together." All those who
were therein made great talk of it among themselves.

The damsel waited for him to speak to her of anything whatsoever until she saw very well and knew that
he would never say a word to her if she did not address
him first, so she said very debonairly: "Lord, whence
came you today?"

"Damsel," said he, "I lay at the abode of a worthy
man in a castle where I had hostel both good and fair,
and it has five strong and excellent towers, one large and
four small; I don't know how to sum up all the work
nor do I know how to name the castle, but I know very
well that the worthy man is named Gornemant de
Goort."

"Ha! fair friend," says the maiden, "Your word
is very fair and you have spoken very courteously. May
God the King be pleased with you. When you called
him a worthy man never did you speak a truer word, for
he is a worthy man, by Saint Richier, this can I indeed
affirm. Know that I am his niece, but I have not seen
him for a long time, and, certainly, since you moved from
your hostel, you have not known a more worthy man, to

my knowledge. He gave you very glad and joyous hostel, for he knew well how to do it, as a worthy man and debonair, powerful and comfortable and rich. But herein there are only six small loaves which an uncle of mine, who is a prior, a very holy and religious man, sent me for supper tonight, and a small keg of mulled wine. There is no other food here except a deer, which a sergeant of mine slew this morning with an arrow."

At once she commands that one set the tables, and they are put in place and the people seated for supper.

They sat very little at their eating, but they took it with great liking. After eating they separated: those remained and slept who had kept watch the night before; those went out who were to keep vigil over the castle that night. There were fifty sergeants and squires who watched that night; the others made great efforts to make their guest comfortable. Those who take charge of putting him to bed place for him fine sheets and very dear coverings and a pillow for his head. The knight had that night all the ease and all the delight that one might know how to devise in a bed, except only the delight of maiden, if it might please him, or of lady, if it were allowed him. But he knew nothing of that, nor did he think of it either little or much, and he soon went to sleep, for he was not worried about anything. But his hostess, who was shut in her room, does not repose; he sleeps at his ease, and she thinks, who has in herself no defense against a battle which assails her. Much does she turn, and much jerk, much does she toss and move about. She has put on a short mantle of scarlet silk over her chemise, and set out on a venture, as a bold and courageous woman, but it is not aimlessly; rather she thinks that she will go to her guest and will tell him a part of her affair. Then she departed from her bed and went forth from her chamber in such fear that all her limbs tremble and her body sweats. Weeping she came from her room and comes to the bed where he is sleeping, and she weeps and sighs very strongly and bows and kneels and weeps so that she wets all his face with tears: she has not the boldness to do more.

So much has she wept that he awakens and is all dismayed and marvels at feeling his face wet, and he sees her on her knees before his bed, who was holding him tightly embraced around the neck, and he did her so much courtesy that he took her in his arms at once and drew her near him. So he said to her: "Fair one, what pleases you? Why have you come here?"

"Ha! gentle knight, mercy! For the sake of God and for His Son, I pray you that you do not hold me more vile because I have come here, although I am nearly naked. I never thought any folly nor malice nor villainy, for there is nothing alive in the world so grieving nor so caitiff that I am not more grieving. Nothing that I have pleases me, for never any day was I without ill, I am so ill-fortuned, nor shall I ever see another night except only this night, nor day except that of tomorrow; rather shall I slay myself by my hand. Of three hundred knights and ten with whom this castle was garnished there are not left herein but fifty; for two hundred and ten less than sixty has a very evil knight, Anguingueron, the seneschal of Clamadeu des Isles, led away and killed and imprisoned. For those who are put in prison I am as grieved as for the slain, for I know well that they will die there, for never again will they come forth. Because of me many worthy men are dead, and it is right that I be discomforted for that.

"Anguingueron has been at siege here before this castle a whole winter and a summer, without moving, and meantime his force grew, and ours has grown smaller and our foods exhausted so that there does not remain in here that on which a bee might feed. We are so entirely beaten that tomorrow, if God does not prevent it, this castle will be given up to him, for it cannot be defended, and I with it as a captive. But, certainly, rather than that he have me alive, I shall slay myself, so will he have me dead; then I do not care if he carries me away to Clamadeu, who thinks to have me: never will he have me, if he has me not empty of life and of soul, in any case, for I keep in a jewel chest of mine a knife of fine steel that I shall thrust in my body. Thus much I had to say to you. Now I shall go on my way again, and I shall let you rest."

Soon the knight will be able to boast if he dare, for never did she come weeping over his face for any other thing, whatever she make him understand, except because she would put in his heart to undertake the battle, if he dare, to defend her and her land. And he said to her:

"Dear friend, show a more cheerful face this night: comfort yourself; do not weep any more, and draw yourself toward me up here, and take the tears from your eyes. God, if it please Him, will do better for you tomorrow than you have said to me. Lie down beside me in this bed, for it is wide enough for our needs; today you will not leave me more."

And she said: "If it pleased you, so would I do."

And he kissed her, who held her grasped in his arms, so has he put her under the coverlet quite softly and wholly at ease and she suffers that he kiss her, nor do I believe that it annoys her. Thus they lay all night, the one beside the other, mouth to mouth, until morning when the day approaches. He solaced her so much that mouth to mouth, arm in arm, they slept until day broke. At daybreak the maiden returned to her chamber. Without serving girl and without chambermaid she dressed and attired herself so that she awoke no one by it. Those who had kept watch during the night, as soon as they could see the day, awakened those who were sleeping and made them rise from their beds, and they got up without delay, and the maiden within the hour repairs to her knight and says to him debonairly:

"Lord, God give you good day today! I believe indeed that you will not make long sojourn here. There will be nothing of staying: you will go away; it does not worry me, for I should not be courteous if it troubled me in any way, for we have given you herein no ease and no good. But I pray God that He may have a better hostel made ready for you where there is more bread and wine and salt and other good than in this one."

And he said: "Fair one, it will not be today that I go seek another hostel. Rather I shall have first put all your land in peace, if ever I can. If I find your enemy out there, it will trouble me if he sits there any longer, because you are grieved for nothing. But if I kill and conquer him I request your love as a reward, that it be mine; no other wages would I take."

She answers graciously: "Lord, you have now asked me for a very poor and despised thing, but if it were contradicted you, you would consider it pride; therefore I do not wish to deny it to you. Nevertheless do not say that I become your friend by such covenant nor by such law that you go to die for me; for it would be too great a pity, for neither your body nor your age is such, know this surely, that you could hold out or suffer strife or battle against so hard a knight nor so strong nor so large as is he who waits out there."

"That you will see," says he, "today, for I shall go fight against him; never will I give it up for any warning." She has built such plea with him that she blames him for it, and yet wishes it; but it often happens that one is wont to conceal one's wish when one sees a man well inclined to do his own liking, so that he may be more pleased to do it. And so she acts wisely, for she has put in his heart that for which she strongly blames him. He asks for his arms. They are brought to him and the gate was opened for him. They arm him and have him mount on a horse that they have made ready for him in the middle of the place. There is no one who does not show that he is worried, and who does not say: "Lord, God be your aid this day and give great ill to Anguingueron the seneschal, who has destroyed all this country."

All the men and women weep as they escort him to the gate, and when they see him outside the castle they all say in one voice: "Fair lord, that true Cross on which God suffered His Son to have pain guard you today from mortal peril, encumbrance and prison, and bring you back safely to a place where you may be at ease, which delights and pleases you!"

Thus they all prayed for him. Those of the host saw him coming and showed him to Anguingueron, who was sitting before his tent and was thinking indeed that they ought to yield the castle before night, or that some one should come forth to fight against him body to body; so he had already laced his hose, and his people were very glad who thought to have conquered the castle and all the country. When Anguingueron sees him, he has himself armed without delay and goes toward him swiftly on a strong and heavy horse and says: "Youth, who sends you here? Tell me the occasion of your way: do you come to seek peace or battle?"

"But you, what are you doing in this land?" says he. "This you will tell me first: why have you slain the knights and confounded all the country?"

Then he answered him proudly and presumptuously: "I wish that this day the castle be voided for me, and the tower yielded, for too long it has been defended against me, and my lord shall have the maiden."

"Accursed today be this news," says the youth, "and he who said it. Rather will it behoove you to cry quits to everything whatsoever that you challenge her."

"Now are you serving me with lies," says Anguingueron; "by Saint Peter, it often comes about that such a one pays the forfeit who has no guilt in it."

This annoyed the youth; so he puts his lance on the felt, and the one spurs against the other without defiance and without speech. Cutting steel and lance of ash had each, large and handy; the horses went very swiftly, and the knights were strong and hated each other to death; so they struck so that they crack boards, they break shields and lances, and the one bears the other down. But they quickly jumped up again and they come together without insults more fiercely than two wild boars and struck each other amid shield and through their tight-meshed hauberks. As much as horses could carry them, by their anger and wrath and by the force of their arms they make the pieces and the splinters of their lances fly in two. Anguingueron fell all alone and was wounded in the body so that he felt it painfully in arm and side. The youth gets down on foot, for he does not know how to seek him out on horse. From the horse he has come to earth, then draws his sword, and passes to attack him. I do not know what more I might describe for you, nor how it befell each one, nor all the blows one by one, but the battle lasted long and the blows were

very hard until Anguingueron fell. He fiercely attacked
him, until he cried mercy to him and the youth says that
there is of mercy not the least. However, he remembered
the worthy man who taught him that he should not knowingly slay a knight after he had conquered him and gained
the upper hand over him. Anguingueron said to him:

"Fair sweet lord, now do not be so proud that you
do not have mercy on me, I promise you well and grant
that now the best of it is yours. You are a very good
knight, but not so good that it would be believed by any
man who had not seen it, and who knew us both, that you
by your arms alone would have killed me in battle; but
if I bear witness of it for you that you have outdone me in
arms in sight of my people before my tent, my word will
be believed and your honor will be known, for never had
a knight a greater. Take care, if you have a lord who has
done you good or service for which he has not had reward,
send me to him, and I shall go there on your behalf and
I shall tell him how you have conquered me by arms
and I shall yield me to him as a prisoner to do whatever
will seem good to him."

"May he have God's hate!" says he, "who seeks
better. Do you know then where you will go? To that
castle, and you will say to the fair one who is my friend
that never in all your life will you be in her harming and
you will put yourself utterly and completely in her
mercy."

He answers: "Then slay me, for she too would have
me slain, for she desires nothing so much as my death
and my sorrow because I had a hand in the death of her
father, and I have done her so much harm that I have
this year taken from her all her knights, either dead or
captured. Evil prison would he have given me who sent
me to her, never would he know how to do worse to me;

but if you have any other friend, either man or woman, who will not have a desire to do me harm, send me there, for she would take my life, if she had me, without fail."

Then he tells him to go to a castle of a worthy man and names him the name of the lord; nor in all the world is there a mason who could better detail the fashion of the castle that he described to him: the water and the bridge he prizes so much for him, and the turrets and the tower and the strong walls around it, until he understands well and knows that he wishes to send him as prisoner to the place where he is most hated.

"There I do not know my protection," says he, "fair lord, where you send me; so help me God, in evil ways and in evil hands do you wish to place me, for in this war I slew for him one of his brothers-german. Slay me, fair sweet friend, rather than make me go to him; there will be my death, if you drive me there."

And he said to him: "Then, you will go into the prison of Arthur the King, and you will greet the King for me and you will tell him in my behalf that he have you see her whom Keu the seneschal struck because she had smiled at me; to her you will yield yourself prisoner and you will say to her, if you please, that may God never let me die until I have taken vengeance for her." He answers that this service he will do him both well and fair. Then the knight who conquered him turned away toward the castle; and he goes to the prison and causes his standards to be carried away, and the host departs from the siege, so that neither brown nor redhead remains. Those of the castle issue forth to meet the one who is returning, but they are greatly annoyed that he had not taken the head of the knight whom he had conquered and handed it over to them. With great joy they dismounted him and disarmed him on a horse block, and say:

"Lord, if you did not bring Anguingueron in here, why didn't you take his head?"

He answers: "Lords, by my faith, I should not have done well, I believe; for he has slain your relatives and I should not be protecting him, rather you would slay him in spite of me. There would have been too little good in me if I had not had mercy on him as soon as I had the best of him; and do you know what the mercy was? He will put himself in the prison of King Arthur, if he keep his pledge to me."

Then the damsel comes, who makes great joy of him and leads him to her chambers to rest and take his ease. She makes him no refusal of hugging and kissing; in place of drinking and eating they play and kiss and hug and talk debonairly.

But Clamadeu who comes thinks folly, and believes to have the castle now without opposition, when a youth uttering great grief met him midway in the road and told him the news of Anguingueron his seneschal:

"In the name of God! Lord, now it goes very badly," says the youth, who makes such grief that he pulls his hair out with his hands, and Clamadeu answers: "In what?"

"Lord," says the youth, "by my faith, your seneschal is conquered in arms, and will yield himself prisoner to King Arthur to whom he goes."

"Come now, youth, who did this, and how could it come about? Whence could the knight come who could make such a worthy man, and so valiant, recreant at arms?"

He answers: "Fair dear lord, I do not know who the knight was, but this much I know of him that I saw him as he came forth from Belrepeire armed with vermilion arms."

"And you, youth, what do you counsel me?" says he, who almost goes out of his mind.

"What, lord? Turn back, for if you went forward nothing indeed would you exploit there."

At this remark there came forward a somewhat white-haired knight who was Clamadeu's teacher. "Youth," says he, "you do not speak worthily; it behooves him to believe wiser and better counsel than yours: if he believes you he will act like a fool, but he will go forward by my advice."

Then he said: "Lord, do you wish to know how you would be able to have the knight and the castle? I shall tell you both well and fair, and it will be very easy to do: within the walls of Belrepeire there is nothing to eat or drink, so the knights are weak and we are both strong and healthy. We have neither thirst nor hunger, so we shall be able to endure a great battle if those within dare to come forth to join us outside here. We will send twenty knights to provoke a battle before the gate. The knight who is disporting himself with Blancheflor, his sweet friend, will want to do chivalry more than he will be able to suffer; and he will be taken or he will die at it, for little aid will be given him by the others who will be weak, and the twenty will do nothing except that they will go deceiving them until we, through this valley, will come upon them so stealthily that we will surround them at the barrier."

"By my faith, I indeed advise this thing that you say to me," says Clamadeu; "we have here chosen men, five hundred knights all armed and a thousand well-attired sergeants, so shall we take them like dead people."

Clamadeu has sent before the gate twenty knights who held displayed to the wind gonfanons and banners of many kinds, and when those of the castle saw them they

opened the gates with abandon, for the youth wished it
thus who before all of them went forth to join the
knights. As a bold man and strong and proud he encounters them all together: whomever he reaches, it does
not seem to him that he is a beginner in arms. That day
the iron of his lance was felt in many a bowel, he pierces
this one's chest and that one's breast, he breaks that one's
arm, and this one's collarbone, this one he kills, that one
he drives mad, that one he knocks down, this one he takes.
The prisoners and the horses he hands over to those who
had need of them, until they see the great battle which had
come up the length of the valley. They were five hundred
counted besides the thousand sergeants who came there,
and the others held themselves near to the gate which was
open. And the others saw the loss of their people driven
mad and dead; so they came straight to the gate all dis-
arrayed and disordered and they held themselves all
lined up close together in their gate and receive them
boldly, but they were few people and weak. The others
grew in strength with the sergeants who had followed
them, until they could not oppose them but withdraw into
their castle. Over the gate there were archers who draw
on the great crowd and the press, which was very ardent
and avid to enter the castle impetuously, until a mass
rapidly has thrust within by force. Those within have
knocked down on those beneath a gate which slays them
and mashes all those that it attains in its fall. Clamadeu
could never see anything for which he might be so
grieving, for the portcullis has killed many of his people,
and shut him out; and he must hold himself in idleness,
for assault in so great haste would be nothing but trouble
wasted. His master who counsels him says to him:

"Lord it is no marvel of a worthy man, if ill befall him: just as it may please and suit God, good and

evil falls to each man; you have lost, that is the sum
of it, but there is no saint who does not have his feast day.
The tempest has fallen on you so your men are maimed
and those within have won, but they will lose again, know
that: pull out both my eyes if they remain in there two
days. Yours will be the castle and the tower, for they will
all beg for mercy. If you can stay here today and tomorrow only, the castle will be in your hand. Even she
who has so often refused you, will again pray you, for
God's sake, that you deign to take her."

Then those who had brought tents and pavilions
there have them spread and the others camped and
lodged themselves as they could. Those of the castle
disarmed the knights that they had taken nor have they
put them in towers or in irons, provided only that they
pledged as knights loyally that they would keep loyal
prison and that they would never seek to do them evil.
Thus they were together therein.

That same day a great wind had driven over the
sea a barge which carried a great load of grain and was
full of other foods. As it pleased God, entire and safe it
came before the castle, and when those within saw it
they send to know and inquire who they are and what they
come to seek. At once those descended from the castle
who went to the barge and ask what people they are,
whence they come and where they are going, and they
say:

"We are merchants who bring food to sell: bread and
wine and salted pork and we have enough beeves and
hogs to kill, if there were need of it."

And they say: "Blessed be God who gave the strength
to the wind which brought you here to port, and welcome
to you! Draw forth: for all is sold as dear as you would
like to sell it. Come quickly to get your wealth, for

you will not be able to disencumber yourself from re-
ceiving nor from numbering plates of gold and plates of
silver that we will give you for the grain and the wine and
the meat. You will have a cart loaded with wealth and
more, if it needs to be done."

Now have those who buy and sell done their tasks
well; they busy themselves with unloading the ship and
have everything from it carried before them to comfort
those within.

When those of the castle saw coming those who were
bringing the provision, you can believe that they had
great joy, and as quickly as ever they were able they
had the food made ready to eat. Now can Clamadeu,
who is musing outside, sojourn a long time; for those
within have oxen and pigs and salted meat in great pro-
fusion and cheese in season. The cooks are not idle; the
boys light the fire in the kitchens to cook the food. Now
can the youth delight himself beside his friend quite at
ease. She kissed him, and he kisses her, so does the one
make joy of the other. The room does not remain quiet:
because of the food all are joyous, for much had they
coveted it. The cooks have hastened so that they cause
those to sit and eat who have great need of it. When they
had eaten, they get up. But Clamadeu and his people
are bursting, who already knew of the good that those
within had. So they say they must go back; that the
castle cannot be starved out by any means: they have besieged the town for nothing.

Clamadeu, who is raging mad, without advice of anyone and without counsel, sends a messenger to the castle
and informs the vermilion knight that until noon of the
next day he will be able to find him alone on the plain to
fight him, if he dares. When the maiden hears this thing
which is announced to her friend she is very grieving and

angered; and he in turn sends word back to him that, since he demands it, he will have this battle, however it may go. Then the grief that the maiden makes grows much stronger and greater. But never for the grief she has of it will he remain, this I believe. Much do all, men and women, beg him not to go combat that one against whom no knight has ever yet had power in battle.

"Lords, now be quiet about it," says the youth, "so will you do well, for I would not leave it for anything nor for any man in the whole world."

Thus he breaks off the talk with them, so that they do not dare to speak to him about it. Rather they go to bed and rest until the morrow when the sun rises, but it grieves them much of their lord that they do not know how to pray him so fair that they may warn him. That night his friend had begged him much not to go to the battle, but to be at peace, for they had no more care about Clamadeu nor his people. But all this availed nothing, and this was a strange marvel, for there was in the flattery great sweetness that she made him, for at each word she kissed him so sweetly and so softly that she put the key of love in the lock of his heart. Never could it be in any manner that she could hold him back so that he should not go to battle. Rather has he called for his arms. He to whom he had intrusted them brought them as quickly as he could. At his arming there was great grief, for it troubled every man and woman. He commended each and every man and woman to the King of Kings, and mounted on his Norse horse which had been brought to him. Then he scarcely remained among them but departed straightway from them and left them uttering their grief.

When Clamadeu sees him coming who was to fight against him, there was in him such foolish thought that he thought to make him empty the bows of the saddle very quickly. The plain was level and fair, nor was there any one but the two of them only, for Clamadeu had removed and sent away all his people. Each one had braced his lance in front of his saddle-bow on the felt, and each spurs to meet the other without defiance and without speech. Cutting steel and lance of ash had each one large and handy. The horses went swiftly and the knights were strong and they hated each other to death. They strike each other so that the boards of the shields crack and the lances break into pieces and the one bears the other down; but they quickly leaped up again and come together on the spot. They combat each other evenly with their swords at great length; I could tell you enough how if I were willing to undertake it, but I wish to take no pains with it, for the reason that one word is worth as much as twenty. Finally Clamadeu was forced to come to mercy against his will, and he granted him all his desire: that he should not put himself for any plea in prison within Belrepeire any more than his seneschal wished to do, nor for all the empire of Rome should he go back to the worthy man's who had the well-placed castle; but he agreed indeed that he would put himself in the prison of King Arthur and that he would tell his message to the maiden whom Keu wounded by his outrage, that he will avenge her, if he has his wish, whoever may have sorrow and grief of it, if God be willing to give him strength for it. Afterward he makes him agree that the next day, before daylight, all those who are within his towers will return healthy and free, nor that ever a day that he have to live will there be a host before the castle, that he will not take it away, if ever he can, nor by his men nor by himself will the maiden have any annoyance.

Thus Clamadeu went away into his own land, and when he came there commanded that all the prisoners should be cast forth from prison so might they go away. As soon as he had said the word his command was obeyed: behold the prisoners drawn forth and they departed, both they and all their harness, for there was not a thing held back. In the other direction, Clamadeu held his way, who travels all alone. It was the custom at that time and we find it written in the letter, that a knight was supposed to put himself in prison with all his attire just as he left the battle where he had been conquered, without having taken away anything or having put on anything. Clamadeu wholly in such guise takes to the road after Anguingueron, who goes toward Dinasdaron, where the King was to hold court.

But on the other side there was great joy in the castle, to which those have returned who had long sojourned in too evil a prison. The whole hall and the lodgings of the knights are noisy with joy. In the chapels and in the minsters all the bells sound with joy, nor is there monk nor nun who does not give thanks to the Lord God. Through the streets and through the squares go caroling every man and woman.

Now there was great delight in the castle, for no one is assaulting or making war on them. But Anguingueron is still going on his way, and Clamadeu after him, and he lay three nights together in the hostels in which he had lain: he followed his traces easily as far as Dinasdaron in Wales where King Arthur in his halls was holding a very high court. They see Clamadeu who was coming in full armor as he was to do; and Anguingueron, who had already delivered at court and told and related his message and had been retained at court both in the household and in council, recognized him. He saw and did not fail to recognize his lord stained with vermilion blood, but said at once:

"Lords, lords, see marvels; the youth with the vermilion arms sends here that knight whom you see; he has conquered him, I am quite certain of it because he is covered with blood. I recognize the blood from here and himself also, for he is my lord, and I his man: his name is Clamadeu des Isles. I believed that there was not a better knight in the empire of Rome, but ill befalls many a worthy man."

Thus Anguingueron spoke until Clamadeu reached there, and the one runs to meet the other and come into the court together.

This was at a Pentecost that the Queen sat beside King Arthur at the head of a dais, and there were there counts and dukes and kings; there were many queens and countesses. It was after all the Masses, and the ladies and the knights had come from the minster. And Keu came into the middle of the hall completely unmantled, and he held in his right hand a stick, on his head a bonnet cap; his hair was blond and was braided in a braid. There was no more handsome knight in the world, but his felonious jests worsened his beauty and his prowess. His tunic was of a rich cloth of silk full colored, he was girded with a wrought belt, the buckle of which and all the parts were of gold. Well do I remember it, for the story thus witnesses it. Each one turns out of his way as he came through the hall. All fear his felonious jests, his evil tongue; so they make way for him, for he is not wise who does not fear felonies too clearly shown, whether it be jesting or be it certain. All those who were therein so much feared his felonious boasts that never did anyone speak to him. In front of all he went to the King there where he was sitting and said:

"Sire, if it pleased you, you would eat now."

"Keu," says the King, "leave me in peace, for, by the eyes in my head, never shall I eat at so great a feast, in order that I may hold a high court, until there come news to my court."

Thus they talked meanwhile and Clamadeu enters into the court, who came to surrender himself as a prisoner at court, armed as he was supposed to come, and said:

"God save and bless the best King who is living, the most noble and the most gentle: so witness all those before whom have been described the great prowesses that he has done! Now hear," says he, "fair sire, for I wish to tell you my message. It grieves me; but none the less I recognize that I am sent here by a knight who has conquered me; prisoner on his behalf I must surrender myself taken to you, for I cannot do better. And if anyone would like to ask me if I know what his name is I should answer him no, but I tell such news of him that his arms are vermilion and you gave them to him, this he says."

"Friend, if the Lord God help you," says the King, "tell me truth if he is in his power free and happy and healthy?"

"Yes, he is, be quite certain of it," says Clamadeu, "fair dear sire, as the most valiant knight whom I ever met, and he told me that I should speak to the maiden who smiled at him, for which Keu did her so great shame that he gave her a slap, but he said that he will avenge it if God grant him the power to do it."

The fool, who hears the word, jumps up with joy and exclaims: "Lord King, if God bless me, she will be well avenged for the buffet, and don't hold it a mockery, for he will have his arm broken for it, never will he know

how to guard himself from it, and his collarbone un-
joined."

Keu, who hears this word, holds it very great foolishness, and know well that he does not refrain from crack-
ing his skull for cowardice, but for the King and for his
shame.

The King has shaken his head over it and said: "Ah!
Keu, I am very grieved that he is not here with me. He
went away on account of you and your foolish tongue,
which grieves me much."

At this word Girflez rises to his feet, to whom the
King commends him, and my lord Yvain, who helps all
those who keep his company, and the King tells them to
take the knight, and conduct him to the chambers, where
the damsels of the Queen are amusing themselves, and
the knight bows to him. Those to whom the King had
commended him have led him to the chambers, and showed him the maiden. He tells her the news such as she
wished to hear it, for she grieved of the buffet which was
seated on her cheek: she had indeed recovered from the
buffet; but she had not at all forgotten nor outlived the
shame, for very wretched is anyone who forgets if anyone
does him shame or ugliness. Grief passes and shame lasts
in a vigorous and courageous man, but in the wretch it
dies and grows cold. Clamadeu has given his message.
Then the King retained him all his life in his court and
household.

He who had delivered from him the land and the
maiden, his friend, the beautiful Blancheflor, beside her
takes his ease and delight. The whole land would have
been his, if it pleased him not to have his heart elsewhere,
but another thing holds him more. He remembered again
his mother whom he saw fall in a faint, and he has a
desire to go see her greater than of any other thing. He

does not dare take leave of his friend, for she objects and forbids him, and sends all her people to pray him earnestly to remain. But there is no use of whatever they say, except that he makes a covenant with them, that if he finds his mother living, he will bring her with him and from then onward he will hold the land, this let them know surely, and if she is dead, the same. Thus he sets out on his way, promising them to come back, and he leaves his friend, the gentle one, very sad and very grieving, and all the others also. When he went forth from the town there was such a procession as though it were Ascension Day or such as on Sunday, for all the monks had gone there cloaked in capes of brocade, and all the veiled nuns, and all of them said:

"Lord, you have drawn us from exile and led us back to our houses. It is no marvel if we grieve when you so soon wish to leave us. Our grief must be very great and it is so great that it cannot be greater."

He says to them: "You must not now weep any longer: I shall return, if God help me, so there is nothing to grieve over. Do you not think it is well that I go to see my mother who lives alone in that wood which is named the Waste Forest? I shall return, whether she is living or not, for never shall I leave her for anything; and if she is alive, I shall make her a veiled nun in your church; and if she is dead, you will hold the service for her soul each year, that God put her with the pious souls in the bosom of Saint Abraham. Lord monks, and you, fair ladies, this ought not to grieve you in any way; for I shall do very great good for you for her soul, if God bring me back."

The Castle of the Fisher King

A T once the monks departed and the nuns and all the others. And he goes away, lance on felt, all armed just as he came there, and all day he held his way, for he encountered no earthly thing nor Christian man nor woman who knew how to teach him the way. He does not stop praying Lord God the sovereign Father that He give him to find his mother full of life and of health, if it is agreeable to His will. This prayer lasted until he came upon a river at the bottom of a hill. He looks at the swift and deep water and does not dare to enter it, and says:

"Ha! Powerful Lord God, if I could pass across this water, I should find my mother beyond, as I think, if she is alive."

Thus he goes along the shore until he approaches a rock, and the water touches that rock so that he could not go forward. At once he saw on the water a boat which was coming from upstream: there were two men in the boat. He stops, and waits for them and thinks that they would go until they came up to him. They both stopped; they remain quiet in the middle of the water, for they had anchored themselves very well; and the one who was in front was fishing with a line and was baiting his hook with a small fish little larger than a grayling. He who does not know what he can do nor in what place he may find passage, greets them, and asks them:

"Teach me," says he, "lords, if there is in this water either ford or bridge?"

Li Contes del Graal, lines 2972-3600.

He who is fishing answers him: "None, brother, by my faith, nor is there any boat, believe me in this, larger than the one in which we are, which would not carry five men, twenty leagues upstream nor down, so one can not get a horse across, for there is neither ferry nor bridge nor ford."

"Then teach me," says he, "for God's sake, where I could have hostel."

He answers: "This and more you would need, I think: I shall lodge you tonight. Go up by that defile which is made in that rock, and when you come to the top you will see before you in a valley a house in which I stay near river and near wood."

At once he goes up until he came on top of the mount; and when he was atop the hill, he looked very far in front of him and saw nothing except sky and earth and said: "What have I come to seek? Nonsense and folly! God give him today evil shame who sent me here: he has now led me astray indeed, for he told me that I should see a house when I should be on top! Fisher, who told me this, you did too great a wrong if you said it to me for evil!"

Then he saw before him in a valley the top of a tower which appeared. One would not find as far as Beirut one so beautiful nor so well placed. It was square, of dark stone. It had two small towers by it. The hall was in front of the tower and the lodges in front of the hall. The youth goes down in that direction and says that he has well sent him who had sent him there, and he voices his approval of the fisher; he does not call him any longer nor disloyal nor lying, as soon as he finds where to lodge. Thus he goes toward the gate. Before the gate he found a drawbridge which was lowered. He went across the top of the bridge and four youths came to meet him. Two disarm him, the third leads away his horse and gives him hay and oats; the fourth dresses him in a new mantle of fresh scarlet. Then they led him to the lodges. Know well as far as Limoges no one might find nor see any so beautiful, if anyone should seek them. The youth stopped in the lodges until he had to come to the lord, who sent two youths for him, and he went with them into the hall, which was square, as long as broad. In the middle of the hall on a couch he saw a handsome worthy man who was partly gray-haired, and his head was covered with marten's fur black as a mulberry, with a purple band on top, and of the same was all his robe. He was leaning on his side, and there was before him a very great fire of dry log, burning brightly, and it was amid four columns. Well might one seat four hundred men around the fire, and each one would have a comfortable place. The columns which supported the chimney were very strong, of thick copper tall and broad. Before the lord went those who are bringing him his guest so that each one was at his side. When the lord saw him coming, he greeted him straightway and said:

"Friend, may it not grieve you if I do not rise to meet you; for I am not able to do so."

"For God, lord, now be silent about that," says he, "for it does not grieve me at all, if God give me joy and health."

The worthy man is so troubled for him that he raises himself up as far as he can and said: "Friend, draw near me here. Don't be dismayed by me; sit here securely beside me, for I so command you."

The youth sat down beside him, and the worthy man said to him: "Friend, from what part did you come to-day?"

"Lord," says he, "this very morning I moved from Belrepeire, thus it is named."

"So help me God," says the worthy man, "too great

a journey have you made today: you must have moved this morning before the watchman had sounded the horn for dawn."

"Rather the first hour had already sounded," says the youth, "I assure you."

While they were speaking thus, a youth enters through the door of the house and brings a sword hanging from his neck, and handed it to the rich man. And he has indeed half drawn it, and saw well where it was made, for it was written on the sword. With this further he saw that it was of such good steel that never could it break into pieces except by one single peril which no one knew except the one who had forged and tempered it. The youth who had brought it said:

"Lord, the golden maiden, your niece, who is so beautiful, has sent you this present: never did you see less heavy of the length and breadth that it has. You will give it to whom it will please you, but my lady would be very glad if it were well employed where it is given. He who forged the sword made only three of them, and he will die, so that never more will he be able to forge any sword after this one.

At once the lord invested him who was a stranger there with that sword by the baldric which was worth a great treasure; the hilt of the sword was of gold, of the best of Arabia or of Greece, the scabbard of orfray of Venice; thus richly equipped the lord handed it to the youth and said:

"Fair lord, this sword was judged and destined for you, and I wish very much that you have it; gird it on, and draw it."

He thanks him for it and girds it on so that he does not fasten it too tightly. Then he drew it naked from the scabbard. When he had held it a little, he put it back again into its sheath; and know well that in a grand manner it fitted his side and better his grasp, and it seemed indeed that in need he would have used it as a valiant man. Behind him he saw the youths standing around the fire which was burning brightly; he saw there the one who was guarding his arms and commended to him his sword, and he kept it for him. Then he sat down again beside the lord, who gave him great honor. Therein there was light as great as one can greatest make of candles in a hostel. While they were talking of one thing and another, a youth came from a chamber, who held a white lance grasped by the middle, and he passed between the fire and those who were sitting on the couch. All those therein saw the white lance and the white iron, and there issued from the iron of the lance a drop of blood, and that vermilion drop flowed as far as the hand of the youth. The youth who had come therein that night saw this marvel, but held himself from asking how that thing came about, for he remembered the warning of the one who made him a knight, who showed and taught him that he should keep himself from too much talking. He fears, if he should ask, that it might be thought villainous of him, therefore he did not ask.

Now two other youths came, holding in their hands candelabra of fine gold, worked in niello. The youths who were bringing the candelabra were very handsome. On each candelabrum were ten candles burning at the very least. A fair and gentle and well attired damsel, who came with the youths, was holding a grail between her two hands. When she had entered therein with the grail that she held, so great a brightness came there that the candles lost their light, just as do the stars when the sun rises, or the moon. After her came another damsel, who held a silver tray. The grail, which went before, was

of fine refined gold; there were precious stones on the
grail of many kinds, of the richest and the dearest there
are on land or sea; those of the grail surpassed all other
stones without a doubt. Just as the lance passed before
the couch, they passed by it and entered from one chamber
into another.

The youth saw them pass and did not dare ask of
the grail whom one served with it, for he always had in
his heart the words of the wise and worthy man. I fear
that there may be harm in that, because I have heard it
related that one can just as well keep silent too much as
speak too much, after all. Whether good or evil befall
him for it, he does not inquire or ask.

The lord commands the youths to bring water and
the table cloths. Those do so who should do it and who
were accustomed to it. The lord and the youth washed
their hands with warm tempered water and two youths
brought a broad table of ivory; as the story witnesses,
it was all of one piece. They held it for a little while
before the lord and the youth, until two other youths
came, who brought two supports. The wood of which the
supports were made had two good graces that the pieces
would last always. Of what were they?—of ebony. Of
a wood for what?—No one indeed can expect that it rot
or burn; it has no care of these two things. The table
was placed on these supports, and the cloth put on top.
But what should I say of the cloth? Legate nor cardinal
nor pope ever ate on so white a one. The first dish was
of a haunch of deer with hot pepper sauce. They lacked
neither clear wines nor juices, with cup of gold for drinking pleasantly. From the peppered haunch of deer a
youth, who had drawn the haunch to him on the silver
tray, sliced before them and put the morsels before them
on a cake which was whole. Meanwhile the grail passed

by in front of them again and the youth did not ask of the grail whom one served with it. He held back because of the worthy man who gently advised him against too much speaking, and he still has his heart on that, and remembers it. But he keeps silent more than is fitting, for at each dish which was served he sees the grail completely uncovered pass in front of him, but he does not know whom they serve with it and he would very much like to know, but he will ask, truly, this he says and thinks, before he turns away, of one of the youths of the court, but he will wait until morning when he takes leave of the lord and of all the other household. Thus he has respited the thing and is intent on drinking and eating. They do not reluctantly bring to the table the dishes and the wines, which are pleasing and delightful.

The eating was both fair and good; with all the foods that king or count or emperor may have was the worthy man served that evening, and the youth together with him. After the meal both spoke together and kept vigil and the youths prepared the beds and the fruit for going to bed. There were some very costly ones: dates, figs, musk nuts, cloves, and pomegranates, and finally electuaries and Alexandrine ginger and pliris aromaticon, resontif and stomaticon. Afterward they drank of many a drink: piment in which there was neither honey nor pepper, and good mulberry wine and clear syrup. Of all this the youth, who had not learned it, marvels much. And the worthy man said to him:

"Friend, it is time to go to bed tonight. I shall go, if it annoy you not, there in my chamber to lie; and when it comes to your pleasure, you will lie outside here. I have no power of myself, so it will be necessary for me to be carried away."

Four slender and strong sergeants at once come

forth from a chamber, they seize by its four corners the cover which was spread on the couch on which the worthy man was lying, and carried him where they should.

With the youth had remained other youths who served him and did whatever was needed for him. When it pleased him, they took off his breeches and undressed him and put him to bed in delicate white cloths of linen.

He slept until morning when the dawn of day had broken and the household had arisen; but when he looked around he saw no one, so he had to get up by himself alone. However much it might grieve him, as soon as he sees that he must do it he gets up, for he can do no better, and dresses himself without waiting for aid and then goes to take his arms. He found them at the head of the dais where they had been brought for him. When he had armed his limbs well, he goes out past the doors of the chambers which that night he had seen opened. But he had his trouble for nothing for he finds them very well closed. He calls and pushes and knocks much: no one opens to him or says a word. When he had called enough he goes to the door of the hall. He finds it open, and descends all the way down the steps and finds his horse saddled and sees his lance and his shield which were leaning against the wall. Then he mounts and goes through the castle, but he finds there none of the sergeants; nor squire nor youth does he see there, so he goes straight to the gate and finds the bridge lowered which had thus been left for him so that nothing would hold him back, at whatever hour he came there, so that he might pass without any stopping. Because of the bridge which he sees lowered, he thinks that the youths have gone away into the forest to look at nets and snares. He has no care to stop longer but said that he would go after them to know if any of them would tell him of the lance why it bleeds, if it can be for any pain, and of the grail where it is carried. Then he goes out through the gate, but before he was down from the bridge he felt that the feet of his horse were raised up on high, and the horse made a great leap, for, if he had not leaped well both the horse and he who was on it would have been badly treated. The youth turns his face to see what this had been, and saw that someone had raised the bridge, so he calls, and no one answers him.

'Come on,'' he says, "you have raised the bridge, now speak to me! Where are you that I do not see you? Come forward, and I shall see you and I shall ask you news of one thing that I should like to know.''

Thus he talks foolishly, for no one wishes to answer him. He makes his way toward the forest and enters into a path and finds that there was a new trace of horses which had gone there.

"I believe," says he, "that those whom I go seeking have gone this way."

Then he rushes through the wood as far as that trace lasts him until he saw by chance beneath an oak a maiden, who is crying and weeping and talking as a miserable, wretched woman:

"Alas!" says she, "wretch that I am! In what a foul hour was I born! The hour that I was engendered be accursed, and that in which I was born, for never before, truly, was I so angered by anything that might happen! I should not be holding my dead friend, if it pleased God, but He would have done a better deed if he were alive, and I were dead. Why did Death, who so discomforts me, take his soul rather than mine? When I see dead the thing that I loved most, what's life worth to me? After him, certainly I don't care about life or my body; now let my soul be thrown out of my body so it may be chambermaid and companion to his, if it deign."

Thus she was uttering her grief of a knight whom

she was holding, who had his head cut off. The youth when he had seen her did not stop until he was in front of her. When he came near, he greeted her, and she him, head lowered, without leaving off her grieving. The youth inquired of her:

"Damsel, who has slain that knight who lies upon you?"

"Fair sir, a knight slew him," says the maiden, "this very morning; but much do I marvel very greatly of one thing that I consider, for one could ride, this they bear witness to, if God keep me, quite straight twenty and five leagues in the direction from which you come, without a hostel's being found which would be either loyal or good or healthy; yet your horse has his sides so full and his hair brushed, if anyone had washed and combed him and made a bed of oats and hay he wouldn't have his stomach better filled nor have his hair better arranged. Of you yourself it seems to me that you have this night been made very comfortable and rested."

"By my faith," says he, "fair one, I had as much ease last night as ever I could, and if it shows, it is with good right, for if anyone should cry out loudly here where we are it would be heard very clearly where I lay last night. You have not known this country very well nor visited all of it; for without any doubt I had the best hostel that I ever had."

"Ha! sir, did you then lie at the castle of the rich Fisher King?"

"Maiden, by the Saviour, I do not know if he is fisher or king, but he is very rich and courteous. Nothing more can I tell you of it except that very late yesterday evening I found two men in a boat, who were gliding along softly. One of the two men was rowing; the other was fishing with a hook, and that one directed me to his house yesterday evening and lodged me last night."

The maiden said: "Fair sir, a king he is, well do I dare say it to you; but he was wounded and maimed without fail in a battle so that he has not been able since to help himself, for he was wounded with a javelin through both his hips. He is still so in anguish because of it that he cannot mount a horse; but when he wishes to disport himself or undertake any amusement he has himself put in a boat and goes fishing with a hook; for this he is called the Fisher King. Thus he takes his pleasure because he could not for anything suffer or endure other sport. He cannot hunt through woods or fields, but he has his falconers, his archers and his huntsmen who go to hunt in his forests; for this it pleases him to dwell in this retreat here, for in all the world there cannot be found a better refuge for his needs, and he has had built such a house as behooves a rich king."

"Damsel," says he, "by faith, true it is what I hear you say, for yesterday evening I heard of this great marvel as soon as I came before him: I held myself above him for a little while and he told me to come to sit beside him, and that I should not hold it for pride, if he did not rise to greet me, for he did not have the ease nor the power, and I went and sat beside him."

"Certainly, he did you very great honor when he seated you beside him. And when you sat beside him, now tell me if you saw the lance of which the point bleeds and yet there is neither flesh nor vein?"

"If I saw it? Yes, by my faith."

"Did you ask why it was bleeding?"

"I never spoke of it."

"So help me God, now know then that you have acted very badly. Did you see the grail?"

"Yes, indeed."

"Who was holding it?"

"A maiden."

"From where was she coming?"

"From a chamber."

"Where did she go with it?"

"She entered into another chamber with it."

"Did anyone go before the grail?"

"Yes."

"Who?"

"Two youths, no more."

"What did they hold in their hands?"

"Candelabra full of candles."

"Who came after the grail?"

"Another maiden."

"What did she hold?"

"A small platter of silver."

"Did you ask the people where they were going thus?"

"Never did it issue from my mouth."

"So help me God, that's so much worse. What is your name, friend?"

He, who did not know his name, guesses and says that he had *Perceval the Welsh* for name, but he does not know if he speaks true or not; but he spoke true, and did not know it. When the damsel heard it, she stood up opposite him and said to him angrily:

"Your name is changed, fair friend."

"How?"

"Perceval the caitiff! Ha! Wretched Perceval, how unfortunate you were then when you did not ask all this, for you would have bettered so much the good king who is maimed, for he would have wholly regained his limbs and would hold his land, and so great good would come of it. But now know that great trouble will you and others have of it. For the sin toward your mother, know this, for she died for grief of you, has it happened to you.

I know you better than you me, for you do not know who I am. I was nourished together with you at your mother's for a very long term. I am your cousin-german and you are my cousin-german, nor does it trouble me less that it has thus mischanced you that you have not known of the grail what one does with it and to whom one carries it, than it does for your mother who is dead or for this knight whom I loved and held very dear for the reason that he called me his dear friend and loved me as a noble, loyal knight."

"Ha! cousin," says Perceval, "if what you have told me is true, tell me how you know it."

"I know it," says the damsel, "as truly as the one who saw her put in the earth."

"Now may God by His goodness have mercy on her soul!" says Perceval.

"You have told me a felonious tale. Since she is put in the earth what should I go forward to seek? For nothing was I going there except for her whom I wished to see. I must hold another way, but if you wished to come with me, I should like it well, for this one who here lies dead will never more be worth anything to you, I pledge it to you: 'The dead to the dead, the living to the living.' Let us go away, you and I, together. It seems to me great folly of you that here alone you watch this dead man; but let us follow the one who killed him, and I promise and grant you either that he will make me recreant or I him, if I can reach him."

She who cannot refrain the great grief that she has in her heart said to him: "Fair friend, at no price would I go away with you, nor would I depart from him until I had buried him. You will hold this metalled road, for by this path departed the evil and proud knight who has slain my sweet friend, but I have not told you because

I wish, so help me God, that you go after him, yet I should like his sorrow as much as if he had slain me. But where was that sword taken which hangs at your left side, which never drew blood from man, and which was never drawn in need? I know well where it was made, and I know well who forged it. See to it that you never trust it; for it will betray you without fail when you come to battle, for it will fly into pieces."

"Fair cousin, one of the nieces of my good host sent it to him yestereve, and he gave it to me and I hold myself well paid with it; but you have much dismayed me, if this is true which you have told me. Now tell me, if you know: if it came about that it should be broken whether it would ever be remade?"

"Yes, but there would be great difficulty. If anyone knew how to keep to the road to the lake which is above Cotoatre, there he could have it rehammered and retempered and made whole. If adventure lead you there, do not go except to Trebuchet the smith; for he made and will remake it, or never more will it be made by any man who may attempt it. Take care that no other put a hand to it; for he would not know how to succeed."

"Certainly, it would be very grievous to me," says Perceval, "if it broke."

Then he goes away, and she remains, not wishing to depart from the dead man for whose death her heart grieves.

The Wretched Maiden

PERCEVAL goes along the path following the tracks until he found a lean and weary palfrey which was going before him at a walk. It was so lean and wretched that it seemed to him that it had fallen into evil hands: it seemed that it had been well worked and badly fed as one does a lent horse, which by day is well worked and at night badly cared for. It was so lean that it trembled as though it were foundered. Its whole nape was split and its ears were hanging down; all the mastiffs and dogs were waiting for entrails and dog food, for it had nothing over its bones except its hide. It had a saddle cloth on its back and a bridle on its head such as befit such an animal. There was a maiden on it: never did anyone see one so wretched. Nevertheless, she might have been beautiful and noble enough, if all were well with her, but so ill was it with her that in the robe she was wearing there was not a handbreath whole, rather her breasts projected from her bosom through the tears. The robe was tied together here and there with knots and coarse sewing, and her flesh seemed hacked just as though it had been done with a scarifier, for it was cracked and burned from heat, from drying and from freezing. She was unlaced and uncloaked, and it showed in her face, where there was many an ugly trace, for tears without stopping had made many a trail on it and descended to her breast and gone flowing over her dress as far as her knees. Anyone who had so much discomfort could have a very grieving heart. As soon as

Li Contes del Graal, lines 3191-4161.

Perceval sees her, he comes toward her at a great pace.
She pulls her clothing around her to cover her flesh; but
she must open holes, for when she covers herself in one
place she closes one hole and opens a hundred.

Perceval has come upon her thus discolored and
stained and wretched, and on overtaking her heard her
dolorously lament her pain and discomfort:

"God!" says she, "may it not please Thee that I
live long thus! I have been wretched too long a time! I
have suffered too much misfortune and it is not through
my desert. God! as Thou knowest well that I have deserved nothing of this, send me, if it please Thee, someone who may cast me forth from this pain, or deliver me
Thou from the one who makes me live in such shame, for
I find no mercy in him, nor can I escape him alive, nor
does he wish to kill me entirely. I do not know why
he desires my company in such manner unless he thus
holds dear my shame and my misfortune. If he knew of
truth that I had deserved it, he ought to have mercy for
it, since I would have paid for it so much, if I might please
him in anything, but certainly I do not please him when
he makes me drag out so harsh a life after him, and he
does not care."

Perceval, who had overtaken her, then said to her:
"Fair one, God save you!"

When the damsel hears him she bows her head and
answers low: "Lord, you who have greeted me, may your
heart have all that it would wish, and yet I have no right
in it."

Perceval who changed color for shame, answered:
"For God's sake, fair friend, why? Certainly, I do not
think nor believe that I ever before saw you nor that I
ever did you any wrong."

"Yes, you did," says she, "so that I am so wretched
and have such sorrow that no one should greet me. It

behooves me to sweat with anguish when anyone stops me or looks at me.

"Truly, I was not aware," says Perceval, "of that misdeed. To do you shame or evil, certainly, came I not here, but my way led me here, and as soon as I had seen you so embarrassed and poor and bare, never more would I have joy in my heart if I should not know the truth of it: what adventure leads you in such grief and pain?"

"Ha! my lord," says she, "thanks! Be silent and flee from here, so let me be in peace. Sin makes you stop here; flee, and you will do wisely."

"This," says he, "I wish to know: for what fear, for what menace shall I flee when no one chases me?"

"Lord," says she, "now let it not worry you, but flee while you still are allowed to, lest Li Orguelleus de la Lande, who asks no thing except battle and combat, come upon us here together. For if he found you placed here, certainly he would slay you in an instant. It is so disagreeable to him when anyone stops me that no one can carry away his head if he arrive in time. Just now he slew one for it; but he first tells each one why he has me in such vileness and put me in such wretchedness."

While they were speaking thus Li Orguelleus came out of the woods, and came like a thunderbolt through the sand and dust crying:

"Truly, in an ill hour did you stop there, you who are standing beside the maiden! Know that your end has come because you have detained her or stopped her for a single step. But I would not slay you until I had related to you for what thing and what misdeed I make her live in such great shame; now listen, and you will hear the tale:

"This year I had gone into the woods and had left this damsel in a pavilion of mine, and I loved nothing except her until by chance it happened that a Welsh youth came there. I do not know what way he went; but so much he did that he kissed her by force, and she made it known to me. If she lied to me, what harm was it to her? And if he kissed her against her will, did he not do afterward all his will? Yes, no one would ever believe that he would kiss her without doing more, for the one thing attracts the other: if anyone kisses a woman, and does no more to her when they are both alone together, then I think there's something wrong with him. A woman who abandons her mouth easily gives the rest, if there is anyone, certainly, intent on it, and well may it be that she may defend herself, and one knows well without any doubt that a woman wishes to conquer everywhere except only in that one melee: when she holds a man by the throat and scratches and bites and beats him, yet would she like to be conquered; she defends herself and yet is impatient. She is so cowardly about granting it, rather she wishes that one do it by force; then she has neither will nor grace. For this reason I believe that he lay with her and he took from her a ring of mine which she was wearing on her finger and he carried it away, which worries me; but first he drank and ate much of a strong wine and of three pastries that I was having kept for me. Now my friend has such courtly fee for it as is manifest. If anyone does a folly, let him so pay for it that he will guard himself from falling into it again. Much could one see me angered when I came back and I knew it, so did I swear much, for I had a right, that her palfrey would not eat oats nor be bled nor shod anew, nor would she have coat nor mantle other than she had at that hour, until I should overcome the man who had forced her, and killed him and cut off his head."

When Perceval had heard him, he answered him word by word:

"Friend, now know without doubt that she has done her penance; for I am he who kissed her against her will, and it troubled her greatly. I took her ring from her finger, nor was there anything more, nor did I anything more. I ate, I assure you, one and a half of the three pastries and I drank as much of the wine as I wanted: in that I did not act foolishly."

"By my head," says Li Orguelleus, "now have you said a wondrous thing who have confessed this. Now have you indeed deserved death when you have truly confessed."

"Death is not yet so near as you believe," says Perceval.

Then they let the horses run the one toward the other, and they come together with such ire that they make splinters of their lances, so that they both empty the saddles, and the one bears the other down; but they quickly leap up again, and draw their naked swords and give each other great blows.

The battle was strong and hard. I have no care to describe it more, for it seems to me pains wasted. But they fight together until Li Orguelleus de la Lande is recreant and asks him for mercy. And he who never forgot the worthy man, who prayed him that he should never slay a knight after he begged mercy of him, said: "Knight, by my faith, I shall never have mercy on you until you have it on your friend; for she had not deserved the evil, this I can swear to you, that you have made her endure."

He who loved her more than his eye said to him: "Fair lord, I am willing to make amends to her as you devise; never could you command anything that I am not ready to do. Of the evil that I have made her have, my heart is very sad and black."

"Go then to the nearest manor," says he, "that you

have around here, and have her bathe peacefully until she is cured and well, then make yourself ready, and lead her well-adorned and well-dressed to King Arthur. Greet him for me and put yourself in his mercy just as you depart from here. If he asks you on whose behalf, you will say to him: on behalf of that one whom he made the vermilion knight by the advice and counsel of my lord Keu the seneschal. It will behoove you to relate at court in the hearing of all who are there the penance and the evil that you have made your damsel endure, so that every man and woman will hear you, and the Queen and her maidens, of which there are some very beautiful ones with her. But above all I prize one of them, for, because she had smiled at me, Keu gave her such a slap on the jaw that he completely stunned her: that one you will seek, I so command you, and you will tell her that I send word to her that I will never enter for any plea into any court that King Arthur has until I shall have so avenged her that she will be joyous and glad of it."

He answers that he will go there quite willingly and will say everything that he has enjoined him; nor will there be any delay except so much that he will first have caused his damsel to rest and adorned her just as she would need; and he would very gladly lead Perceval himself there to take his rest, to cure and to take care of his cuts and his wounds.

"Now go, may you have good fortune," says Perceval, "and think of her: I shall seek hostel elsewhere."

The conversation ceases at once; neither one of them waits there any longer, but they separate without more discussion. That night he had his friend bathe and dress richly, and he made her so comfortable that she came back into her beauty. Afterward they both held their way straight toward Carlion where King Arthur

was holding court; but it was very privately, for there
were only three thousand valiant knights. In sight of all,
he who came and brought his damsel went to surrender
himself as a prisoner to King Arthur, and said when he
was before him:

"Sire," says he, "I am prisoner to do whatever you
wish, and indeed is it reason and right, for thus I was
commanded by the youth who asked vermilion arms of
you and had them."

Just as soon as the King heard him he understands
well what he meant. "Disarm youself," says he, "fair
sir! May he who made of you a present to me have joy
and good adventure, and may you be welcome! For him
you will be held dear and honored in my hostel."

"Sire, it behooves me to say something else," says
he, "before I am disarmed; but in any case I should like
for the Queen and her maidens to come to hear the
news that I have brought here to you; for it will not be
told until that one has come here who was struck on the
cheek for a single smile that she had made; for never
was there any other misdeed."

Thus he ends his word. When the King heard that
it behooves him to summon the Queen before him, he
sent for her, and she comes there and all her maidens
come there hand in hand, two by two.

When the Queen was seated beside her lord, King
Arthur, Li Orguelleus de la Lande said to her: "Lady,
a knight whom I esteem much, who has conquered me by
his arms sends you greetings. I do not know what more
I may say of him except that he sends you my friend,
this maiden who is here."

"Friend, great thanks to him!" says the Queen.

And he tells her all the vileness and the shame that
that he had long done to her and the pain that she had
endured and the occasion for which he did it; he told her

everything without concealing anything. Afterward they showed him her whom Keu the seneschal struck, and he said to her:

"He who sent me here, maiden, prayed me that I should greet you for him, and that I should never move my feet until I had told you that never, may God help him, will he enter, for anything that may befall, into any court that King Arthur may hold until he has avenged you for the slap and for the buffet which was given you for him."

When the fool heard this, he leaps to his feet and cries out: "Lord Keu, if God bless me, you will pay for it truly, and soon."

After the fool, the King says in turn: "Ha! Keu, you did not act courteously to the youth when you mocked him. By your mockery, you have taken him from me so that never more do I think to see him."

Then the King has his prisoner knight sit before him, and pardons him his imprisonment and then commands him to be disarmed. And my lord Gauvain, who sat on the King's right, asks, "For God, sire, who can this be who alone by his arms conquered so good a knight as is this one? For in all the Isles of the Sea I have not heard a knight named, nor did I see him nor did I know him who might compare with this one in arms or in chivalry."

"Fair nephew, I do not know him," says the King, "and yet I have seen him; but when I saw him I did not even ask him a thing, and he told me that I should make him a knight right on the spot. I saw him handsome and proper so I said to him: 'Brother, gladly; but dismount meanwhile until they have brought you some arms all gilded.'

"And he said that indeed he would not take them,

nor would he ever get down on foot until he had vermilion arms. And he said other marvels: that he did not wish to have arms except those of the knight who was carrying off my golden cup. Keu, who was annoying, and still is and always will be, and never wishes to say any good, said to him: 'Brother, the King gives you the arms and hands them over to you, go at once and take them.'

"He who did not know how to understand the jest thought that he was speaking true, and went after him and slew him with a javelin that he hurled at him. I do not know how they began the melee nor the massacre but that the Vermilion Knight of the Forest of Quinqueroi struck him, I do not know why, with his lance, and acted haughtily. The youth struck him right in the middle of his eyes with a javelin of his and killed him and had the arms. Since then he has served me so well that, by my lord Saint David, whom they adore and pray in Wales, never more in chambers nor in halls two nights in turn will I lie until I see him, if he is alive, on sea or on land; rather will I move ever to go seek him."

As soon the the King had sworn this, all were assured that there was nothing except to go. If anyone had then seen clothes packed and covers and pillows, chests filled, pack horses trussed and carts and vans loaded, for they do not take too few tents and pavilions and shelters. A wise and well lettered clerk could not write in a day all the harness and all the attire which was made ready at once. Thus as though moving out with his army, the King departs from Carlion and all the barons follow him; not a maiden remains there whom the Queen does not take with her for festivity and lordliness. That night they are lodged beside a forest in a prairie.

Three Drops of Blood on the Snow

IN the morning it had snowed well, for the country was
very cold. Perceval had risen early in the morning
as he was wont, for he wished to seek and encounter
adventure and chivalry, and he came straight into the
prairie, which was frozen and snow covered, where the
King's host was lodged. But before he came to the
tents, a flock of wild geese flew which the snow had
dazzled. He saw them and heard them, for they were
going away noisily because of a falcon which came drawing after them at a great rate until he found abandoned
one separated from the flock, and he struck it so and
bruised it that he knocked it down to earth. But it was
too early, and he left it, for he did not wish to entangle
himself with it. Perceval begins to spur there where he
had seen the flight. The goose was wounded in the
neck, and bled three drops of blood which spread out on
the white and seemed natural color. The goose had no
harm nor hurt which might hold it against the ground
until he might come there in time; she had flown away
previously.

When Perceval saw the trampled snow on which
the goose had lain, and the blood which appeared around,
he leaned upon his lance and looked at that image, for
the blood and the snow together seemed to him like the
fresh color which was on the face of his friend, and he
thinks until he forgets himself; for the vermilion seated

Li Contes del Graal, lines 4162-4602.

on the white was on her face just the same as these
three drops of blood on the white snow. In the looking
that he was doing, it seemed to him, it pleased him
so much, that he saw the new color of the face of his
beautiful friend. Perceval muses over the drops; he
uses up the whole dawn at it, until squires came forth from
the tents who saw him musing and thought that he was
drowsing.

Before the King awakened, who was still sleeping
in his tent, the squires encountered Sagremor, who by his
disarray was called Desreez, in front of the King's
pavilion. "Come on," says he, "do not hide it from me,
why do you come here so early?"

"Lord," say they, "outside this host we have seen
a knight who is dozing on his charger."

"Is he armed?"

"In faith, yes."

"I shall go speak to him," says he, "and I shall bring
him to court."

Straightway Sagremor runs to the King's tent and
wakes him: "Sire," says he, "out there is a knight dozing
on that plain."

The King commands him to go, and with that he
tells him and prays him that he bring him to him, and not
leave it.

At once Sagremor commands that his horse be brought
out for him and called for his arms again. It was done
as soon as he commanded it, and he has himself armed
well and quickly. Fully armed he issues from the host
and goes to the knight. "Lord," says he, "it behooves
you to come to court."

He does not move and makes it seem that he does
not hear him. He begins to say it again, and he does not
move, and he becomes angry and says:

"By Saint Peter the Apostle, you will come there in spite of yourself. I am worried that I ever begged you, for I have badly used my speech. Then he has displayed the ensign which was wound around his lance, and the horse beneath him springs forward, and he seizes land on one side and he tells him to guard himself for he will strike him, if he does not take care. Perceval looks toward him and sees him coming at a gallop. Then he left his thinking entirely, and comes in turn spurring to meet him. When the one encounters the other, Sagremor shatters his lance, that of Perceval neither breaks nor bends, rather he thrusts at him with such force that he knocked him down in the middle of the field. The horse without stay goes away fleeing, head raised, toward the tents, and those saw him who were getting up throughout the tents, and it annoyed much those who were there.

Keu, who could never keep himself from saying felony, makes fun of him and says to the King: "Fair sire, see how Sagremor is coming back! He holds the knight by the bit and leads him against his will."

"Keu," says the King, "it is not good that you so mock worthy men. Now go there, and we shall see how you will do better than he."

"Sire," says Keu, "I am very glad it pleases you for me to go there, and I shall bring him without fail quite by force, be he willing or not, and I shall make him name his name."

Then he has himself fully armed. He is armed and mounts and goes away to the one who was so intent on the three drops he was looking at that he had no care for anything else. Keu cries to him from very far: "Vassal, vassal, come to the King! You will come there indeed, by my faith, or you will pay heavily for it."

Perceval, who hears himself threatened, turns the

head of his horse and spurs with his steel spurs the horse, which does not go slow. Each one desires to do well and they come together without any ruse. Keu strikes so that his lance breaks and shatters like a piece of bark, for he put all his force in it. Perceval does not pretend, he strikes him high on the buckle and knocks him down on a rock so that he dislocates his collarbone, and so that he breaks the bone of his right arm between the elbow and the armpit like a dry splinter, just as the fool foretold who many times had divined it; true was the fool's divination. Keu faints from the distress and his horse goes fleeing toward the tents at a full trot. The Bretons see the horse which is coming back without the seneschal, and youths run to horse, and ladies and knights move. When they find the seneschal fainted, they believe indeed that he is dead. Then began very loud grieving that every man and woman made over him. And Perceval leaned again on his lance over the three drops; but the King was greatly worried over the wounded seneschal, he is grieving and wrathful until he is told not to be dismayed, for he will get well, provided he have a physician who knows how to undertake to put the collarbone back in its place and to make broken bone retake.

The King, who had a tenderness for him and loved him much in his heart, sends to him a very wise physician and three maidens from his school who set his collarbone and they have bound his arm and set the shattered bone. Then they carried him to the King's tent and comfort him much and tell him that he will get well; never should he be discomforted about anything, and my lord Gauvain says to him: "Sire, if the Lord God help me, it is not reasonable, well do you know it, as you yourself have always said and rightly judged, that a knight should as those two have done, take another knight from his thought, whatever it may be. If they were wrong, that I do not know, but ill has befallen them for it, that is a certain thing. The knight was pensive of some loss that he had had, or his beloved was taken away from him and he is troubled by it, and was thinking of it. But if it were your pleasure I should go to see his countenance and if I found him at such point that he had forsaken his thought, I should say to him and I should pray him that he come to you here."

At this word Keu became angry and said: "Ha! my lord Gauvain, you will bring the knight here by the hand, however much it may annoy him. It will be done, if he lets you and you have the power. Thus have you taken many of them: when the knight is weary and has had enough of arms, then must a worthy man request the gift that one let him go conquer him. Gauvain, may my neck have a hundred curses, if you are a bit so foolish that one may not learn from you! Well do you know how to sell your words, which are very fair and polished. Great outrages and great felonies and great annoyance will you say to him indeed. May he have the ill will of God who believed it and who believes that I might be in it! Certainly, you could do this task in a silk bliaut; never will it behoove you to draw sword or to break lance. For this can you esteem yourself that, if your tongue does not fail you to say: 'Lord, God save you and may He give you joy and health!' he will do your will. I am not saying anything to teach you; but you will know how to stroke him well, just as one strokes a cat, and people will say: 'Now my lord Gauvain is fighting fiercely.'"

"Ha! lord Keu," says he, "more fairly might you say it to me. Do you think to avenge your ire and your evil disposition on me? I shall bring him, by my faith, if ever I can, fair sweet friend, and I shall not have my arm hurt for it, and without dislocating a collarbone, for I do not like such pay."

"Now go there for me, nephew," says the King. "You have spoken very courteously. If it can be, bring him here; but take all your arms, for you shall not go unarmed."

He who had repute and renown for all good qualities, had himself armed at once, and mounted on a strong and nimble horse, and came straight to the knight, who was leaning on his lance. He was not yet weary of his thought, for it pleased him greatly. Nevertheless the sun had melted two of the drops of blood which were seated on the snow and was melting the third; because of this the knight was not thinking as much as he had done.

My lord Gauvain draws toward him walking quite softly, without making any felonious indication, and says: "Lord, I should have greeted you, if I had known your heart as well as I do my own; but so much can I tell you indeed that I am messenger to the King, who sends word and prays you through me that you come to speak to him."

"There have already been two of them here," says Perceval, "who took from me my joy and wished to lead me away just as though I had been taken; and I was so pensive of a thought which much pleased me. He who wanted to part me from it was not looking for my advantage; for before me in this place there were three drops of fresh blood which illuminated the white. On looking at it, it seemed to me that I saw there the fresh color of the face of my beautiful friend, and indeed I did not wish to depart from it."

"Certainly," says my lord Gauvain, "this thought was not base but was courtly and gentle, and he was foolish and haughty who removed your heart from it. But now I desire greatly and covet to know what you will be willing to do. I should gladly, if it displease you not, lead you to the King."

"Now tell me, fair dear friend, first," says Perceval, "if Keu is there, the seneschal?"

"By my faith, truly he is there, and know well that it was he who just now jousted with you. The jousting cost him so much that you have broken his right arm, and yet you do not know it, and dislocated his collarbone."

"Then have I," says he, "well avenged the maiden whom he struck."

When my lord Gauvain heard him, he marvels at it and starts and says: "Lord, if God save me, the King was seeking none other than you. Lord, what is your name?"

"Perceval, lord, and yours what?"

"Lord, know truly that the name I have in baptism is Gauvain."

"Gauvain?"

"Truly, fair lord."

Perceval rejoiced much at this and said: "Lord, well have I heard speak of you in many places and the acquaintance of the two of us I desired much to have, if it sit not ill with you."

"Certainly," says my lord Gauvain, "it pleases me not less than it does you, but more, I believe."

And Perceval answers: "By my faith, then I will go, for it is right, willingly where you wish, and I shall now act much more agreeable because I am your acquaintance."

Then the one goes to embrace the other, and they

begin to unlace helms and coifs and ventails and draw up
their mails, then they go away joyously. At once youths
who, from an outpost where they were, saw them enjoying
each other's company, ran and have come before the
King:

"Sire, sire," say they, "by faith, my lord Gauvain
is bringing the knight here, and the one is showing great
joy of the other." There is no one who hears the news
who does not rush out of his tent and go to meet them,
and Keu says to the King, his lord:

"Now has my lord Gauvain, your nephew, the prize
and the honor of it. The battle was very perilous and
grievous, if I am not lying; for he returns just as healthy
as he moved out, for never did he receive there another's
blow nor any other feel blow of his; not by a single word
did he give him the lie, so it is right that he have the
glory and praise for it and that it be said that he has done
that in which we were not able to succeed, and yet we
put in it all our powers and efforts."

Thus, were it right or wrong, Keu said his will just
as he was wont. My lord Gauvain does not wish to lead
his companion to court armed, but all unarmed. He has
him disarmed in his tent, and one of his chamberlains
brings him a robe out of his chest, he presents it and offers
it to him to wear.

When he was dressed both well and fair in tunic and
mantle, which was very good and fitted him well, they
both come hand in hand to the King, who sat before his
tent.

"Sire, sire, I bring you," says my lord Gauvain to the
King, "the one whom, as I believe, you would see very
gladly: for the entire past fortnight, it is he of whom you
talked so much, it is he whom you went seeking. I hand
him over to you, see him here."

"Fair nephew, great thanks to you!" says the King, to whom he is so welcome that he leaps to his feet to meet him and says: "Fair lord, welcome! Now I pray you that you inform me how I shall call you."

"By faith, never shall I conceal it from you, fair sire King," says Perceval; my name is Perceval the Welsh."

"Ha! Perceval, fair sweet friend, since you have put yourself in my court, never more will you depart from it, my wish. Much have I had great grief of you, when I saw you first, that I did not know the improvement that God had destined to you, yet it was very well divined so that all my court knew it through the maiden and the fool, whom Keu the seneschal struck. You have well made their divination true from start to end. Of this no one is now in doubt, for of your chivalry I have heard true news."

The Queen came at this word, who had heard the news of his coming. As soon as Perceval saw her and it was told him that it was she and there came after her the damsel who smiled when he looked at her, at once he went to meet them and said:

"God give joy and honor to the most beautiful, to the best of all the ladies there are, witness all the eyes who see her and all those that have seen her!"

The Queen answers him: "May you be welcome here as a proven knight of high and fair prowess!"

Then Perceval again greeted the maiden, the one who smiled at him, and embraced her and said to her:

"Fair one, if you had any need I would be the knight who would never fail you in aid."

The maid thanks him for it.

The Quest for the Grail and the Lance

G REAT was the joy that the King and the Queen and
the barons made of Perceval the Welsh. They lead
him to Carlion; for they returned there that night, and
all night they make great joy, and the next day they did
likewise, until the third day that they saw there a damsel
who came on a tawny mule and held in her right hand a
whip. The damsel was tressed with two tresses twisted
and black; and if the words the book relates are true,
never was anything of so ugly description born even within hell: Never did you see iron so black as were her neck
and hands. But yet that was the least compared to the
other ugliness she had: her eyes were two holes, small
also as rat's eyes; her nose was of monkey or cat, and
her lips of donkey or ox; her teeth resembled yolk of
egg in color, they were so orange, and she had a beard
like a goat; in the middle of her chest she had a hump,
toward the spine she resembled a shepherd's crook and
she had back and shoulders too well made to lead balls, and
she had a hump on her back and twisted legs that were
like two willow ropes: well was she made to lead the
dance! The damsel advances on her mule as far as
in front of the King; never before had any such maiden
come to any king's court. She greets the King and the
barons all together except Perceval only, and said on
her tawny mule:

Li Contes del Graal, lines 4603-4746.

"Ha! Perceval, Fortune is bald behind and hairy in front. May he have God's ill will who greets you and who prays or begs any good for you! Why did you not hold on to Fortune when you encountered her! You entered the Fisher King's, you saw the lance which bleeds; and was it then such pain for you to open your mouth and to speak that you could not ask why that drop of blood leaps through the point of white iron? And of the grail that you saw you did not ask nor did you inquire what noble man was served with it. He is very unfortunate who sees such beautiful times that none is better fitting, and still waits for fairer to come. It is you, the unfortunate, who saw that it was time and place to speak, yet you kept silent. You had great leisure for it; in evil time did you keep so silent; for, if you had asked it, the rich king, who is much dismayed, would have been wholly cured of his wound, and would hold his land in peace which he will never have more. Do you know what will happen to the king who will not hold land nor be cured of his wounds? Ladies will lose their husbands for it, lands will be ravaged for it, and maidens disconsolate, who will remain orphans, and many knights will die for it; all these evils will come about because of you."

Then said the damsel to the King: "King, I am going away, may it not annoy you, for it behooves me still this night to take my hostel far from here. I do not know if you have heard the Chastel Orguelleus spoken of; but tonight it behooves me to go there. In the castle there are five hundred and sixty and six knights of renown; and know that there is not a one who does not have with him his friend, a gentle woman, courteous and beautiful. I tell you the news of it because no one who goes there will fail to find jousting or battle; whoever wishes to do chivalry, if he seeks it there, will not lack it. But if anyone would like to have the esteem of the whole world, I think I know the place and the piece of ground where it could best be conquered, if there were anyone who dared to do it: at the hill which is beneath Montesclaire there is a damsel besieged. Much honor would he have conquered who could take away the siege and deliver the maiden, and he would have all the praises, and he to whom God would give such good fortune could gird on quite safely the Sword of the Strange Baldric."

The damsel at once became silent, who had well said what pleased her, and departed without saying more. My lord Gauvain leaps up and says that he will do his best to rescue her and will go there, and Girflez the son of Do says in turn that he will go, if God help him, before the Chastel Orguelleus.

"And I on Mont Dolereus," says Kahedin, "will go mount and I will not stop before reaching there."

Next Perceval says quite differently that he will not lie in a hostel two nights in all his life, nor will he hear news of strange passage without going there to pass, nor of knight who is worth more than another knight or more than two, without going to combat him, until he knows of the grail whom they serve with it, and until he has found the lance which bleeds, and until the proven truth is told him why it bleeds; never will he leave it for any pain.

Indeed thus as many as fifty have risen for this, and the one promises the other and says and swears that he will not know of marvel or adventure without going to seek it in however felonious land it may be.

Gauvain's Adventures

WHILE they were dressing and arming themselves in the middle of the hall, Guinganbresil enters through the door of the hall and brings a shield of gold. On the shield there was a band of azure; the third of the shield was the band in full measure and quite proper. Guinganbresil recognized the King, and greeted him as he should, but he did not greet Gauvain; rather he accused him of felony and said:

"Gauvain, you killed my lord, and you struck him without ever defying him. Shame and reproach and blame have you for that; so I accuse you of treachery; and may all the barons know well that I have not erred by a word." At this word my lord Gauvain, quite shamed, leaped to his feet, and Agrevain li Orguelleus, his brother, jumps up and pulls him and said to him:

"For God, fair lord, do not shame your lineage. From this blame, from this shame that this knight puts on you I shall defend you, that I promise you."

And he said: "Brother, never will any man except me defend me from it, and I must defend myself because he accuses no one but me of it. But if I had done anything wrong to the knight, and I knew it, very willingly would I seek peace with him and I would make him such amends that all his friends and mine would have to hold it well done; and if he has said his outrage, I deny it and offer my gage either here or there or where it will please him."

Li Contes del Graal, lines 4747-6216.

And he says he will prove him guilty of ugly and villainous treason at the end of forty days before the king of Escavalon, who is fairer than Absalom, in his mind and opinion.

"And I," says Gauvain, "pledge you that I shall follow you right now, and there we shall see who will have the right."

At once Guinganbresil turns away and my lord Gauvain dresses himself to follow without delay. Whoever had good shield, whoever good lance, whoever good helm and good sword presented it to him; but it did not please him to carry anything of another's; he leads seven squires with him and seven chargers and two shields. Before he had moved away from court, there was very great grief made after him, many a breast beaten, many a hair pulled and many a face scratched; indeed there was no lady so sensible who does not utter great grief for him; great lament do many men and women make. And my lord Gauvain goes away.

Of the adventures that he found you will hear me tell at great length.

He sees first a group of knights pass across the plain and he asks a squire who was coming all alone after them and who was leading with his right hand a Spanish horse and who had a shield at his neck: "Squire, tell me who those are who are passing here?

And he answers: "Lord, that is Meliant de Liz, a worthy and bold knight."

"Are you his?"

"Lord, not I. My lord is named Traez d'Anet, who is worth no less than he."

"By faith," says my lord Gauvain, "I know Traez d'Anet well. Where is he going? Do not conceal anything of it from me."

"Lord, he is going to a tournament that Meliant de Liz had taken against Tiebaut de Tintaguel, and you will go there too, my wish, in the castle against those outside."

"God!" says my lord Gauvain then, "but was Meliant de Liz not nurtured in the house of Tiebaut?"

"Yes, lord, if God save me; for his father loved Tiebaut much as his man and believed him so much that on his death bed, where he lay, he commended his little son to him. And he nurtured and guarded him as dearly as he could, until he knew how to pray and entreat the love of a daughter of his; and she said that she would grant him love on no day until he should be a knight. He who wished to act quickly had himself made a knight at once; then he came back to his prayer.

" 'It can not be in any manner,' says the maiden, 'by my faith, until you have before me done so much in arms and jousted so much that my love shall have cost you; for the things that one has for a jest are not so sweet nor so pleasing as those that one pays for. Take a tourney with my father, if you wish to have my love; for I wish to know without doubt if my love would be well seated, if I had put it on you.'

"Just as she dictated, he has undertaken the tournament; for love has such great lordship over those who are in its power that they would not dare to refuse anything that one might deign to command them. And you would be very negligent if you did not put yourself in it, for they would have great need of it, if you were willing to aid them."

And he said to him: "Brother, go away, follow your lord, and you will do wisely, so let stand what you are saying."

At once he departed, and my lord Gauvain goes on

his way; he does not cease traveling toward Tintaguel, for
he can not pass elsewhere. Tiebaut had gathered all his
relatives and his cousins and had summoned all his
neighbors, and they had all come there, both high and
low, young and white-haired. But Tiebaut had not
found in the advice of his privy council that he should
tourney against his lord; for they were very much afraid
that he might want to destroy them wholly, and he had
had all the entries of the castle walled up and covered.
The portals were well walled with hard stone and mortar,
so that there was no other entry except a little postern,
the door of which was not of alderwood: they had failed to
seal it. The door was to last always: it was of copper
fortified by a bar; on the door there was a load of iron
such as a cart might carry. My lord Gauvain came toward the door after all his harness; for he had to pass
this way or turn back, for there was no other way nor
other cart road for seven great leagues. When he sees
the postern closed, he enters into a meadow beneath the
tower which was closed around with stakes. He dismounted beneath an oak and hung his shields on it. The
people of the castle see him, many of whom were greatly
grieved over the tourney which was put off. But there
was an old vavassor in the castle, well endowed and wise,
powerful in land and lineage, nor was he misbelieved
about anything that he might say, however it might go
in the end. He had seen those who were coming, for
they were pointed out to him at a distance. Before they
had entered the closed meadow, he went to speak to
Tiebaut and said:

"Lord, if God save me, I have, as I think, seen two
knights of the companions of Arthur the King who come
here: two worthy men hold a very great place, for only
one would win a tourney. I should advise, as for my-

self, that you should go toward the tournament quite
surely, for you have good knights and good sergeants
and good archers, who will kill their horses; and I
know well that they will come to tourney before this door.
If their pride brings them here, we shall have the gain
of it, and they the loss and the hurt."

By the advice that he gave, Tiebaut has given leave
that all those who wished should arm themselves fully
and go out. Now the knights are joyous, the squires run
for the arms and the horses, and put saddles on them.
And the ladies and the maidens go to sit in the highest
places to see the tournament, and they saw beneath them
on the plain the harness of my lord Gauvain, and they believed at first that there were two knights, because they
saw two shields hung on the oak. And the ladies who
were born at a good hour, when they had mounted, say
that they will see these two knights who will arm themselves before them.

Thus the ones conversed, and there were those who
said: "God! fair lord, this knight with so much harness and so many chargers that two would have enough
with them—if he has no companion with him, what will
he do with two shields? Never was a knight seen who
carried two shields together; for this it seems to me a
great marvel if this knight who is alone will carry both
these shields."

While they were speaking thus, and the knights were
going out, the oldest daughter of Tiebaut, who had caused
the tourney, had mounted high in the tower. With the
oldest was the smallest, who dressed herself so grace-
fully with sleeves that she was called the Maiden with
the Little Sleeves, for she had them imprinted on her
arms.

With the two daughters of Tiebaut, ladies and maidens
mounted to the top. The tournament assembles now

before the castle; but there was none so capable as
Meliant de Liz was, witness his friend, who was saying
to the ladies all around her:

"Ladies, truly no knight that I might see pleased me
so much before, I don't know why I should lie to you about
it, as Meliant de Liz does. Then is it not solace and
delight to see so good a knight? He must well sit on
a horse and bear lance and shield who knows how to
disport himself so fairly with them."

Her sister, who was sitting beside her, told her there
was one more handsome. She was very angry at this,
and got up to strike her. But the ladies pull her back,
and held her and delayed her so that she could not touch
her, which annoyed her greatly.

The tournament begins, in which many a lance was
broken and many a sword blow struck and many a knight
beaten down. But know that it costs him too dear who
jousts with Meliant de Liz; for no one lasts before him
whom he does not carry to hard ground; and if his lance
shatters, he employs a great sword stroke, and he does
it better than all those on either side, so his friend has such
great joy that she cannot hold herself, and says:

"Ladies, see marvels: never did you see his equals,
nor did you ever hear them spoken of. See the best
youth that you might ever see with your eyes, for he
is fairer and does better than all those who are in the
tourney."

And the little one said: "I see a fairer and better,
perhaps." She at once comes to her and says, as inflamed
and heated:

"You brat, you were so bold that by your malad-
venture you dared to blame any creature that I had
praised? And now take this slap, and keep yourself
from it another time."

Then she strikes her so that she sealed all her fingers

on her face. The ladies who are beside her blame her very much for it and pull her away. Then afterward they speak again of my lord Gauvain among themselves: "God!" says one of the damsels, "this knight beneath that hornbeam, what is he waiting for that he does not arm himself?"

Another more arrogant said in turn: "He has sworn the peace."

And another said after her: "He is a merchant; don't say again that he is to wait to tourney: he is leading all those horses to sell."

"Rather he is a changer," says the fourth, "he has no inclination to divide today with the poor knights that wealth that he bears with him. Don't think that I am lying to you: it is money and silverware in those sheaths and in those trunks."

"Truly, you have too evil tongues," says the little one, "and you are wrong. Do you think that a merchant would carry lances as big as this one carries? Certainly, you have done me deadly hurt who have said such deviltry. Faith that I owe the Holy Spirit, he seems a better tourneyor than a merchant or changer: he is a knight and well does he resemble one."

And all the ladies together say to her: "Then, fair friend, if he resembles one, he is not. But he makes himself resemble one because he thinks thus to steal costumes and passages. He is a fool, and yet he thinks to be wise, for in this way he will be taken, will be accused as a thief and blamed for villainous and foolish theft and he will have a halter around his neck for it."

My lord Gauvain hears this mockery clearly and understands that the ladies talk of him, and he has great shame and great annoyance for it; but he thinks, and he is right, that he is accused of treason, and he must go to defend himself; for if he did not go to the battle as he has an agreement, he would have shamed first himself and then all his lineage. And because he was in dread that he might be hurt or taken, he has not joined in the tourney, and he has very great desire to do so, for he sees the tournament, which keeps on growing stronger and better. And Meliant de Liz calls for large lances to strike better. All day until evening was the tourney before the portal. Whoever makes gain there, he carries it where he thinks to have it safe.

The ladies see a very tall and bald squire, who was holding a lance shaft and carrying a crownpiece on his neck. One of the ladies, silly and foolish, calls to him at once and says:

"Dan squire, if God help me, now are you a very senseless fool, who in that press snatch those lance irons and those crownpieces and those broken shafts and those cruppers, and you do as a good squire: whoever rushes in there holds himself little dear, and I see here very near you in this meadow beneath us wealth without guard and without defense. Fool is he who does not think of his advantage, while he can. And see the most debonair knight who was ever born! For if anyone plucked all his whiskers he would not move. Now do not hold gain so vile, but take all the horses and all the wealth, and you will do wisely, for never will anyone defend it against you."

Straightway he entered the meadow and struck one of the horses with his shaft and said: "Vassal, are you not then hale and hearty who keep watch here all day, nor have you done anything here, neither pierced shield nor broken lance?"

"Go on," he says, "how does it concern you? The reason why it does not happen I hope you will indeed know soon; but by my head, it will not be now, for I should not deign to tell it to you. Now flee from here, and hold your way and go do your task."

At once he goes away from him, nor was he such that he would dare then to speak of anything which might grieve him. And the tournament ceases; but there was many a knight taken in it and many a horse killed, and those outside had the prize, and those within gained there and on parting pledged each other that they would re-assemble the next day on the field and would tourney.

Thus they parted that night; then all those who had come out of the castle re-entered it. And my lord Gauvain was there, who entered it after the crowd. Before the portal he met the worthy man, the vavassor, who that day gave the advice to his lord to begin the tourney, and he very debonairly and fairly begged him to lodge, and said: "Fair lord, in this castle is your hostel all prepared. If it please you, sojourn here today, for, if you went ahead, you would not have good hostel any more today; for this I pray you remain."

"I shall remain, thank you, fair lord," says my lord Gauvain, "for I have heard much worse said."

The vavassor, speaking of one thing and another, leads him away, and asks him to what it was due that he had not that day borne arms with them in the tourney. And he told him all the why: that he is accused of treason, and he must guard himself from prison and from wounds and hurt until he can put himself outside the blame that is put upon him, for he could shame himself and all his friends by his delay, if he could not come on time to the battle that he has undertaken.

The vavassor praised him much for it and said that he was grateful to him for it: if he had left the tourney for this, he had done right. Thus the vavassor leads him to his house and they dismount.

The people of the court are intent on accusing him

harshly, and they hold a great parley on how the lord may go take him. And his elder daughter tries all that she can and knows how, because of her sister whom she hates:

"Lord," says she, "I know well that you have lost nothing today, rather I think you have gained much more than you know, and I shall indeed tell you how: in an ill hour will you do anything except command that one go take it. Never will he dare defend it who brought it into the town, which he serves with very evil guile: he has shields and lances brought and horses led on the right, and thus he steals costumes because he resembles a knight, and he acts noble in this guise when he goes trading. But now give him his desert for it; he is at the house of Garin, the son of Berte, at the hostel, who has lodged him. Just now he went this way; for I saw that he was leading him there."

Thus indeed she strove to have him caused shame. The lord mounts at once, for he wishes to go there himself: he makes his way straight toward the house where my lord Gauvain was. When his little girl sees that he is going there in this manner, she goes out through a door behind, for she has no desire that anyone see her, rather she goes quickly and the straight way to the hostel of my lord Gauvain at the house of Dan Garin, the son of Bertain, who had two very beautiful daughters. When the maidens see that their little lady is coming, it behooves them to rejoice over it, and they do so without pretense: each one has taken her by the hand, and they lead her in joyfully, kissing her eyes and mouth. But Dan Garin, who was neither poor nor wretched, had mounted again, and his son Bertran with him, and they both went away to the court as they were wont, for they wished to speak to their lord, and they meet him in the middle of the street. The vavassor greets him, and asks him where he was going. And he told him that he wanted to go to disport himself in his house.

"By faith, that ought not harm me," says Dan Garin, "nor displease, and you could see there now the handsomest knight on earth."

"By faith, I am not going to seek that," says the lord, "rather shall I have him taken: he is a merchant, and he leads horses to sell and pretends to be a knight."

"Ha! here is a too villainous speech," says Garin, "that I hear you say: I am your man, and you my lord; but I here give you back your homage, for myself and all my lineage I defy you here and now, rather than that I should suffer you to do wrong to this one in my hostel."

"Rather I had no desire to do so," says the lord, "so help me God, neither your guest nor your hostel will have anything but honor from me, not because, by my faith, it has not been well counseled and admonished to me."

"Great thanks," says the vavassor, "and it will be very great honor to me if you will come to see my guest."

The one takes his place at the other's side at once and they go until they came to the hostel where my lord Gauvain was. When my lord Gauvain, who was very well taught, sees them, he gets up and says: "Welcome!" They both greet him, then they sit down beside him.

Then the worthy man, who was lord of the country, inquired of him why he had held himself back that day, since he had come to the tourney, that he had not tourneyed. And he did not deny it to him that he might have had neither hurt nor shame; but straightway after he tells him that a knight was accusing him of treason, and he was going to defend himself against this charge in a royal court.

"You had legitimate motive," says the lord, "without any fail, but where will this battle be?"

"Lord," says he, "I am to go before the king of Escavalon for it, and I am going there quite straight, I believe."

"I shall hand over to you escort," says the lord, "which will lead you. And because you will have to pass through many a poor land, I shall give you victuals to carry and horses that will carry them."

My lord Gauvain answers that he has no need to take them; that if any can be found for sale, he will have victuals in plenty and good lodgings, wherever he may go, and everything whatsoever he will need; for this reason he seeks nothing of his.

At this word, the lord departs. At parting he saw coming in the other direction his little girl, who at once embraced my lord Gauvain by the leg and said: "Fair lord, hear this; for I have come to appeal to you of my sister who has beaten me, so do me right of her for it, if you please."

My lord Gauvain kept silent, for he did not know what she said, but he put his hand on her head. The damsel pulls him and says: "I say to you, fair lord, that I appeal to you of my sister, whom I do not hold dear nor do I love her, because she has done me great shame today because of you."

"Fair one," says he, "of what concern is it to me? What right can I do you in this?"

The worthy man, who had taken leave, hears what his daughter asks, and says: "Daughter, who commands you to come to appeal to knights?"

And Gauvain says: "Fair dear lord, is she your daughter then?"

"Yes, but don't ever worry about her words," says the lord, "she is a child, a silly thing and foolish."

"Certainly," says my lord Gauvain, "then I should be too great a villain, if I did not do her will. Tell me, however," says he, "my sweet and debonair child, what right I could do you of your sister, and how?"

"Lord, only so much that, if it please you, you will, for the love of me, bear arms in the tourney tomorrow."

"Tell me then, dear friend, if you ever before made entreaty to any knight for any need?"

"No, my lord."

"Don't have any concern for her," says the father, "whatever she may say, don't listen to her folly."

And my lord Gauvain says to him: "Lord, if the Lord God help me, rather has she said too good a childish speech as so small a maiden, nor shall I ever refuse her, but if it pleases her, tomorrow I shall be her knight for a while."

"Thanks to you, fair dear lord!" says she, who has such joy of it that she bowed low to his feet.

At once they part without saying more. The lord carries his daughter away on the neck of his palfrey, and asks her why this dispute had arisen. She told him clearly the truth of it from beginning to end and said:

"Lord, I was very grieved by my sister, who testified that Meliant de Liz was the best and handsomest of all, and I had seen that knight down there in the meadow, and I could not leave off without telling her in opposition that I saw there a handsomer than he; for this my sister called me a foolish brat and pulled my hair, and cursed be anyone whom that pleases!

"I should let both my braids be cut off me to the nape of my neck, by which I should be much worsened, by covenant that tomorrow at day that knight would beat down Meliant de Liz in the fray; and then would be fallen the cry that my lady makes of him. Today she has held such great plea of him that she annoys all the ladies; but 'great wind falls with little rain.' "

"Fair daughter," says the worthy man, "I command and give you leave, because it will be a courtesy, to send him some token of love, either sleeve or wimple."

She, who was very simple, says: "Very gladly, when you say so; but my sleeves are so small that I wouldn't dare to send one to him. Indeed, if I sent it to him, he would esteem it nothing."

"Daughter, I shall think very much of it," says the father, "now you be quiet about it; for I can do it very easily."

Thus speaking he carries her away in his arms, and she has great solace because he hugs her and holds her until he comes before his palace. When the other sister saw him coming and holding her before him, she had great annoyance from it in her heart and said: "Lord, whence comes my sister, the Maiden with the Little Sleeves? Indeed, she knows much of turns and tricks; she is very ready for them. But from where have you brought her?"

"And you," says he, "what do you want to do about it? You should indeed keep quiet about it; for she is worth more than you are, who have pulled her tresses and beaten her, which grieves me much; you have not acted courteously."

Then was she very discomfited because of her father, who had spoken to her this reproach and this insult. And now he had a vermilion samite drawn from one of his coffers, and he has had a very long and broad sleeve cut and made from it; then he called his daughter and said to her:

"Daughter, now get up tomorrow morning and go to the knight, before he moves. By love you will give him this new sleeve, and he will carry it to the tourney when he goes there."

And she answers her father: as soon as she sees the clear dawn she will be, her wish, awake and up and dressed.

The father departs at this word. She, who has great joy of it, prays all her companions that they do not let her sleep long in the morning, but awaken her hastily as soon as they see the day, if they wish to have her love. And they did so very well indeed, for as soon as they saw the dawn break in the early morning, they had her dress and get up.

The maiden rose early and all alone went to the hostel of my lord Gauvain; but she did not come there so early that they had not already risen, and had gone to the minster to hear Mass that was sung for them. The damsel remained at the home of the vavassor until they had prayed long and heard all that they should. When they returned from the minster, the maiden leaps up to meet my lord Gauvain and says:

"God save you and give you honor this day! But for my love wear this sleeve that I hold here."

"Willingly, thank you, my friend," says my lord Gauvain.

After this the knights did not delay arming themselves; armed they gather outside the town, and the damsels and all the ladies of the castle have gone up again on the walls, and they saw assemble the throngs of strong and bold knights. Before all, Meliant de Liz came into the ranks at a full gallop and had left his companions quite far, a rod and a half. When the elder girl sees her friend, she can not hold her tongue, but says:

"Ladies, see coming the one who has the prize and lordship of knighthood."

My lord Gauvain moves as much as horse can carry him toward the other who does not dread him, but breaks his lance completely to pieces. My lord Gauvain strikes him so that he does him very great grief, so that he carries him straightway to the plain and holds out his hand to the horse, takes it by the bridle and hands it over to a youth and tells him to go to the one for whom he is tourneying, and to tell her that he is sending her the first gain that he has made this day, that he wishes her to have it. The youth leads the horse with the saddle to the maiden, who from a window of the tower where she was had seen Dan Meliant de Liz fall, and said:

"Sister, now you can see Dan Meliant de Liz lying, whom you were prizing so. Whoever knows how ought to prize rightly: now it appears as I said yesterday; now one sees well, if God save me, that there is such a one there who is worth better."

Thus knowingly she goes contradicting her sister so that she drives her out of her senses, and she says: "Brat, be quiet! For if I hear you sound another word of him today, I'll give you such a slap that you will not have a foot that will hold you up."

"Ha! sister, let you remember God"; says the little damsel, "because if I have told you the truth, you ought not to beat me for it. By faith, I saw him indeed beaten down, and you just as well as I did, and it doesn't seem to me that he has power to get up yet. And if now you were to burst for it, I shall say it anyhow, for there is no lady here who doesn't see him somersault and lie quite flat."

Then the other would have given her a slap, if she had been suffered to do it; but the ladies who were around would not let her strike her. Meanwhile they see coming the squire who was leading the charger with his right hand. He found the maiden sitting at a window and presents it to her. She gives him more than sixty thanks for it and has the horse taken. And he goes to deliver the thanks to his lord, who seemed to be lord and master of the tournament; for there is no knight so skillful, if he attacks him with the lance, that he does not take from him his stirrups. Never was he so eager to gain chargers: he gave four that he gained during the day by his hand as presents, and he sent the first of them to the little damsel; with the other he pays his debt to the wife of the vavassor, who was much pleased by it; one of his two daughters had the third, and the other had the fourth.

The tournament breaks up, and they come back in through the gate. My lord Gauvain carries away the prize on both sides; nor was it yet midday when he departed from the strife. On his return my lord Gauvain had so great a throng of knights that the whole town was full of them, and all those who followed him wished to inquire and ask who he was, and of what country. He met the maiden right at the door of his hostel, and she never did anything else but at once she caught him by the stirrup and greeted him and said to him:

"Five hundred thanks, fair very sweet lord!"

He knew well what she meant, and answered her nobly:

"Rather would I be gray and white, friend, than that I should be recreant in serving you, wherever I may be: never shall I be so far from you, if I know your need, that torments keep me from coming at the first message."

"Great thanks!" says the damsel.

Thus he and she were talking when her father came into the palace, who with all his might begs my lord Gauvain to remain the night and to take his hostel; but first he requests and prays him to tell him his name, if it pleases him. My lord Gauvain excuses himself from remaining and says to him:

"Lord, I am called Gauvain; never was my name concealed in any place where it was sought of me, nor did I ever yet say it, if it were not first asked of me."

When the lord heard that it was my lord Gauvain, his heart was very full of joy, and he said to him:

"Lord, now remain, tonight take my service; for I have not as yet served you in anything, nor did I ever in my life see a knight, this I can swear to you, whom I should like as much to honor."

He begged him much to remain, and my lord Gauvain has denied all his prayer. The little damsel, who was not foolish or bad, takes him by the foot and kisses it and commends him to the Lord God. My lord Gauvain asks her what she intended by that. And she answered that she had kissed his foot with the intention that he should remember her in whatever place he might come. And he said to her:

"Do not doubt it; for, so help me God, fair friend, never more shall I forget you when I depart from here."

At once he parts from them and takes leave of his host and the other people, and they all commend him to God.

That night my lord Gauvain lay at a cloister and he had there everything he needed. Early in the morning he went riding along the way until he saw, in passing by, beasts that were feeding beside the edge of a forest. He told Yonet to stop, who was leading one of his horses, the very best, and was holding a very stiff and strong lance. He tells him to bring him the lance and to saddle his horse for him, the one he is leading by his right hand, and to take his palfrey and lead it for him. He does not remain on that one; for Yonet has without delay handed

over to him the horse and the lance, and he turns away
after the does, and makes after them so many twists and
turns that he overtook a white one beside a briarpatch
and put his lance across its neck. The doe leaps like a
stag, and escapes him, and he after, and he chased it
until he might have caught and held it if his horse had
not cleanly lost the iron from one of its front feet. And
my lord Gauvain sets out after his gear on the road, for
he feels that his horse would give way beneath him, and
he is greatly worried by it; but he does not know what
made him limp if a stake has not wounded him in the
foot. At once he calls Yonet, and commands him to
dismount and to take care of his horse, which is limping
very strongly. He does his command, and lifts up its foot
and finds that an iron is lacking, and says:

"Lord, it is necessary to shoe it, so there is nothing
to do but to travel quite softly until we can find a smith
who can reshoe him."

Then they traveled until they saw people who came
forth from a castle and traveled along a road. In front
there were people on an excursion, boys on foot who were
leading dogs, and hunters came after, carrying trenchant
spears; after, there were bowmen and sergeants carrying
bows and arrows. Behind them came knights; after all
the knights there came on two chargers two others, one of
whom was young, gentle, and fair above all the others.
That one alone greeted my lord Gauvain and took him
by the hand and said:

"Lord, I retain you. Go there whence I came, and
stop at my houses. Today it is indeed time and season
to take lodging, if it trouble you not. I have a very
courteous sister, who will make great joy of you; and
this one, lord, whom you see here beside me will lead
you there."

Then he said: "Go, I send you, fair companion, with this lord. Lead him to my sister. Greet her first, then tell her that I send word to her by the love and by the great faith that should be between her and me, that, if she ever loved a knight, she should love this one and hold him dear, and that she make as much of him as of me who am her brother: let her give him such solace and such company that it grieve him not, until we have returned. When she has retained him with her debonairly, follow us hastily; for I should like to return to keep her company as soon as I am able."

The knight departs then, who conducts my lord Gauvain there where all hate him to death. But he is not known there, for he was never seen there before, and he does not think to have any care there. He looks at the site of the castle, which was sitting on an arm of the sea, and saw the walls and the tower so strong that it fears nothing, and he looks at the whole town peopled with very fair people and the exchanges all covered with gold and silver and with monies, and sees the places and the ways all full of good workers, who did as many diverse trades as trades are different: this one makes helms and that one hauberks, and this one saddles and that one blazons, and this one bridles and that one spurs, and these furbish swords, these full cloths and those weave them, these comb them and those shear them, and the others melt gold and silver, these make rich and beautiful works: cups, goblets, and bowls and jewels worked in enamels, rings, belts and buckles; well could one think and believe that there was a fair every day in the town, which was full of so much wealth, of wax, of pepper, of kermes, and of green and gray furs, and of all merchandises.

Looking at all these things and lingering from place to

place, they have gone until they were at the tower, and youths come out, who received all the horses and the other gear. The knight enters into the tower alone with my lord Gauvain and leads him by the hand as far as the maiden's room and says to her:

"Fair friend, your brother sends greetings to you, and of this lord commands you that he be honored and served, and do not do it unwillingly, but with as very good heart as though you were his sister and he were your brother. Now take care that you do not be miserly in doing all his will, but generous and noble and debonair. Now think of it, for I am going away, for it behooves me to follow him to the wood."

And she who has great joy says: "Blessed be he who sent such company as this! Whoever lends me so fair a companion does not hate me; thanks be to him. Fair lord, now come and sit here," says the maiden, "beside me! Because I see you fair and gentle, and for my brother who begs it of me, I shall make you good company."

At once the knight turns away, for he does not sojourn with them more. And my lord Gauvain remains, who does not complain of the fact that he is alone with the maiden, who was very courteous and beautiful, and was so well taught that she does not think to be watched because she is alone with him. They both speak of love; for if they were to speak of anything else, they might mix themselves in great foolishness.

My lord Gauvain requests and prays her love and tells her that he will be her knight all his life. She does not refuse him, but agrees willingly. Meanwhile a vavassor entered therein who harmed them much, who knew my lord Gauvain, and found them kissing each other and making great joy of each other. As soon as he saw that joy, he could not hold his mouth quiet, but cried out with great force:

"Woman, may you be shamed! May God destroy
and confound you; for the man in all the world whom
you ought to hate most you allow thus to have pleasure
with you, and he kisses and hugs you! Wretched and
foolish woman, you do well what you ought to do, for
you ought to draw his heart from his belly with your
hands rather than with your mouth. If your kissing
touches his heart, you have drawn his heart from his
belly; but you would have done much better if you had
torn it out with your hands, for thus you ought to do. If
a woman is to do anything good, in this one there is nothing of a woman who hates evil and loves good: he is
wrong who then calls her a woman, for there she loses
the name when she loves anything except good. But
you are a woman, well do I see it; for he who sits beside you killed your father, and you kiss him. When a
woman can have her ease, little does she care for the
rest."

At this word he jumps back, before my lord Gauvain
might have said either more or less to him. And she falls
to the pavement in a faint. My lord Gauvain seizes her
and lifts her up from it pale and green from the fear that
she had had. When she had recovered, she said:

"Ha! now are we dead! Because of you I shall die
wrongly today, and you, I believe, for me. Now there
will come here, as I believe, the people of this town: soon
there will be more than ten thousand of them amassed
before this tower. But herein there are plenty of arms
with which I shall arm you very quickly: one worthy man
could defend this hole from a whole host."

Now she who was not secure runs to take arms.
When she had armed him well with the armor, both she
and my lord Gauvain feared less, except that there was so
much misfortune there that he could not have a shield,
so he made a shield of a chessboard and said:

"Friend, I do not wish you to go seek another shield for me."

Then he threw the chessmen on the ground; they were of ivory, ten times as large as other chessmen and of harder bone. From now on, whatever may come, he will think to defend the door and entry of the tower, for he had girded on Escalibor, the best sword there was, for it cuts iron like wood. And he who had gone out had found sitting side by side an assembly of neighbors, the mayor and the aldermen and other burghers in great numbers, who had not taken poison, for they were both big and fat. And he came there at more than a walk, crying:

"Now to arms, lords, and we will go take the traitor Gauvain, who slew my lord."

"Where is he?—Where is he?" says this one and that one.

"By my faith," says he, "I found him, Gauvain, the proven traitor, in that tower where he takes his ease, and hugs and kisses our lady, and she does not refuse him anything, but rather allows it and is indeed willing. But now come, and we shall go take him. If we can hand him over to my lord, we shall have indeed served him to his liking. The traitor has well deserved to be dragged out with shame; nevertheless, take him alive, for my lord would rather have him alive than dead, and he would not be wrong, for a dead thing fears nothing. Alarm the whole town, and do what you ought to do."

At once the mayor got up and all the aldermen after. Then might you see furious villeins who take axes and halberds; this one takes a shield without straps, that one a door and this one a winnow. The criers cry the ban, and all the people come together. The holy bell of the community rings so that no one remains; there is no one so wretched who does not take fork or flail or pike or mace; there was not such noise in Lombardy to assail the snail; there is no one so little that he does not go there, and who does not carry some arm there. Behold my lord Gauvain dead, if the Lord God does not counsel him! The damsel makes ready to aid him boldly and calls out to the community:

"Hu, hu!" says she, "low rabble, mad dogs, stinking servile pack! what devils have summoned you? What are you seeking? What are you asking? May God never give you joy! So help me God, you will not take away the knight who is in here, rather if it please God, there will be I don't know how many dead and crushed. He did not fly in here, nor come by a hidden way, but my brother sent him to me as a guest, and I was much entreated by him that I should act with him just as I should do with my brother himself. Do you hold me a peasant for it if I by his request give him company, joy and solace? Whoever wishes to hear, let him hear it, for never did I make him joy for else, nor did I think of any other folly. For this I bear you greater ill will when you do me such great shame that you have drawn your swords on me at the door of my chamber, and you don't know how to say why. And if you know how to say it, you have not spoken to me of it, so it appears to me as very great insolence."

While she was speaking her mind, those who were with force breaking the door to pieces with axes which they were holding, have split it into two halves. But the porter who was within has defended it against them very well, for with the sword which he was holding he paid the first so that the others are dismayed by it, nor does anyone dare to step forward. Each one guards his own affair, for each one fears for his head: no one so bold comes forward who does not fear the porter so much; never will there be such a one who will thrust his hand forward nor take a step forward. The damsel very angrily hurls at them the chessmen that are lying on the floor, and she gritted her teeth and scratched her face, and swears like a mad woman that she will have them all destroyed, if ever she can, before she dies. But the villeins are stubborn and boast that they will beat down the tower on them, if they do not surrender. And they defend themselves better and better with the great chessmen that they hurl at them. Most of them flee backward, for they can not suffer their assault, and with pikes of steel they dig at the tower as though to tear it down, for they do not dare to attack or fight at the door, which is well forbidden them. Of the door, if it please you, believe me that it was so narrow and so low that two men could not enter there except with difficulty; for this, one worthy man could well dispute and defend it. To split to the teeth and to brain unarmed villeins it was not necessary to call a better porter than was there.

Of all this the lord who had lodged him did not know a word, but he came back as soon as he could from the wood where he went to hunt. Still those were picking around the tower with pikes of steel. Meanwhile behold Guinganbresil, who by I know not what adventure came into the castle at a great pace, and was greatly dismayed at the hue and the hammering that he heard the villeins doing. Of the fact that my lord Gauvain was in the tower he did not know a word. But when it came about that he knew it, he forbade that there should be any one so bold there, whoever he might be, as he held his body dear, who should dare dislodge a stone, and they said that they would not leave off anything of it because of him, but rather they would beat it down on his own body this day, if he were inside with him. When he sees that his forbiddance will avail nothing, he considers that he will go to meet the King and will bring him to this disorder which the burghers have begun. And the King was just coming from the wood, and he meets him and tells it to him:

"Sire, your mayor and your aldermen have done you great shame, who have been attacking your tower since this morning and are tearing it down. If they do not pay for it and buy it, I shall bear you very ill will. I had charged Gauvain with treason, well do you know it, and it is he whom you have had lodge in your quarters, and it would be indeed right and reason, since you have made him your guest, that he should not have shame or outrage there."

The King answers Guinganbresil: "Master, he will not have as soon as we arrive there. Of the fact that this has befallen him I am greatly annoyed and it grieves me strongly. If my people hate him to death, I must not be angered by it, but from taking and wounding his person, for my honor, I shall guard him because I have lodged him."

Thus they come to the tower and find the people around, who are making a very great uproar. He tells the mayor to go away and lead the people away. They go away, so that no one remains there, not even one, since it pleased the mayor.

In the place there was a vavassor, a native of the town, who counseled all the country, for he was of very great sense.

"Lord," says he, "now ought one to counsel you well and faithfully: it is not to be marveled at if he who did the treason of your father whom he slew has been assailed here, for he is hated to death thus rightly as you

know.   But the fact that you have lodged him must protect and guard him that he be not taken here or die here,
and if anyone does not wish to lie about it, Guinganbresil
whom I see there, who went to the court of the King to
accuse him of treason, must save and guarantee him.   This
is not to be concealed that he had come to defend himself
from it in your court; but I advise him to take a respite of this battle for a year, and that he go to seek
the lance of which the iron bleeds always, never will it be
so wiped that a drop of blood hang not from it: either
he hand over that lance to you or he put himself again
at your mercy in such prison as he is here.   Then you
will have better occasion to hold him in prison than you
would have right now.   Never would you know how,
this I believe, to put him in so grievous pain that he
would not know how to overcome it.   By whatever one
can and knows, ought one to grieve what one hates: to
torture your enemy I do not know how to counsel you
better."

The King holds to this counsel.   He comes to his
sister in the tower and found her very angry.   She got
up to meet him; and my lord Gauvain also, who does not
change color nor tremble for any fear that he may have.
Guinganbresil comes forward and has greeted the maiden,
who had changed color, and said three words in vain:

"Lord Gauvain, lord Gauvain, I had taken you here
in safe conduct, but at least I told you that never should
you be so bold that you should enter into the castle nor in
any city that my sire had if it should please you to turn
aside from it.   Of what has been done to you, you need
now offer no contention."

And the wise vavassor said: "Lord, if the Lord God
help me, all this can one indeed amend.   From whom
can one demand anything if the townspeople have as-

sailed him? The trial would not be ended before the great day of justice. But it will be done according to the wish of my lord the King who is here; he commands me and I say it: provided it be agreeable to both you and him, take respite for a year of this battle, and let my lord Gauvain go away, provided he will take an oath of my lord: that he will hand over to him within a year without more term the lance whose point sheds tear of the quite bright blood that it weeps, and so is it written that there will be an hour when all the kingdom of Logres, which was formerly the land of the ogres, will be destroyed by that lance. Of this my lord the King wishes to have oath and pledge."

"Certainly, I should first," says Gauvain, "let myself die or languish here seven years before I would make that oath or would pledge you my faith on it. I do not have such fear of my death that I do not like better to suffer and endure death in honor than to live in shame and perjury."

"Fair lord," says the vavassor, "indeed, it will not be dishonor for you, nor ever, as I believe, would you be worse for it in a sense that I wish to say: you will swear that you will do your best to seek the lance; if you do not bring back the lance you put yourself back in this tower, so will you be quit of the oath."

"True," says he, "as you say it, am I ready to make the oath."

They have now brought forth to him a very precious sanctuary, and he has made the oath that he will put all his effort in seeking the lance which bleeds.

Thus the battle is left, respited for a year between him and Guinganbresil. He has escaped from great peril when he is freed from this one. Before he issued forth from the castle he took leave of the maiden and told all his youths that they should go back to their land and lead back all the horses except the Gringalet.

The youths depart from their lord weeping and go away. Of them and of the grief that they make it does not please me to say anything more.

Of my lord Gauvain the tale here is silent where it is, and speaks of Perceval.

Perceval and the Hermit

PERCEVAL, this the story tells, has so lost his memory that he no longer remembers God. Five times April and May passed, that is five entire years before he entered into a minster or adored God or His Cross. Thus he remained five years, nor for this did he leave off seeking chivalry and strange adventures, the felonious and harsh ones he went seeking and found so many of them that well did he prove himself, never did he undertake anything so grievous in which he did not well succeed. Within the five years he sent sixty knights of worth to the court of King Arthur as prisoners. Thus he employed the five years that he never remembered God. At the end of the five years he happened to be making his way through a wilderness, as he was wont, armed with all his arms, when he encountered three knights with ladies as many as ten. They had put their heads in their hoods and were all going on foot and in rags and barefoot. Of him who was coming armed and was holding lance and shield the ladies marveled much, because for salvation of their souls they were doing their penance on foot for the sins that they had done. One of the three knights stops him and says:

"Fair dear lord, then do you not believe Jesucrist who wrote the new law and gave it to the Christians? Certainly, it is neither reasonable nor good to carry arms, rather it is great wrong, on the day that Jesucrist died."

Li Contes del Graal, lines 6217-6518.

And he who had no span of day nor of hour nor of time, there was so much sorrow in his heart, answers: "What day is it then today?"

"What day, lord? You don't know? It is the adored Friday, the day that one ought to adore the Cross and weep for his sins, for today was He hung on the Cross who was sold for thirty deniers. He who was pure of all sins saw the sins by which the whole world was bound and imbued: He became a man for our sins. True it is that God and man was He; that the Virgin gave birth to a son, whom she conceived by Holy Spirit, in whom God received both flesh and blood, so was His deity covered in flesh of man. That is a certain thing, and whoever will not believe Him thus, never will he see Him in the face. He was born of the Virgin lady and took the form and the soul of man with the holy deity, who on such a day verily, as today is, was put on the Cross and drew from hell all his friends. Very holy was that death which saved the living and resuscitated the dead from death to life. The evil Jews (whom one ought to kill like dogs) by their envy did their evil and our great good when they raised Him on the Cross; they lost themselves and saved us. All those who believe in Him ought today to be in penitence: today ought no man who believes God to carry arms either in field or way."

"And whence come you now thus?" says Perceval.

"Lord, from here, from a good man, a holy hermit, who lives in this forest, nor does he live, he is such a very holy man, except of the glory of heaven."

"For God, lords, what did you do there? What did you ask, what did you seek?"

"What, lord?" says one of the ladies, "we asked counsel of our sins and took confession there; we did there the greatest task that any Christian can do who wishes to turn closer to God."

What Perceval had heard made him weep, and it pleased him that he should go speak to the holy man: "I should like," he says, "to go to the hermit, if I knew how to hold to the path and the way."

"Lord, if anyone would wish to go there, let him hold this path quite straight, just as we have come, through this thick and narrow wood, and let him take care of the branches which we knotted with our hands when we came through there. We made such signs there in order that no one should go astray who might go toward the holy man."

At once they commend each other to God, nor do they ask each other anything more. Perceval enters into the path sighing from the heart in his bosom because he felt he had done wrong toward God, for which he repented. Weeping much he goes toward the wooded grove and when he came to the hermitage he dismounts and disarms himself, he attaches his horse to a hornbeam, then he enters the hermit's. In a little chapel he found the hermit and a priest and a young cleric, this is the truth, who were beginning the service, the highest which can be said in holy church, and the sweetest. Perceval puts himself on his knees as soon as he enters the chapel and the good man calls to him who saw him simple and weeping, for flowing as far as his chin the water was dripping from his eyes. Perceval, who feared much to have done wrong toward God, took the hermit by the foot and bows to him and hands joined prays him that he give him counsel, for he has great need of it, and the good man commanded him to say his confession, for he will never have remission if he is not confessed and repentant.

"Lord," says he, "it is indeed five years since I knew where I was, nor did I love God nor believe God nor did I do anything except evil."

"Ha! fair friend," says the worthy man, "tell me

why you have done this, and pray God that He have mercy on the soul of his sinner."

"Lord, I was once at the home of the Fisher King, and I saw the lance of which the iron bleeds without a doubt, and of that drop of blood which I saw hang from the point of the white iron, nothing did I ask of it; never afterward, certainly, did I make amends. And of the grail that I saw there I did not know whom one served with it, and I have since had so great grief of it that I would have been dead, my wish, and I forgot Damedeu for it, so that never since did I cry to Him mercy nor did I do anything that I knew by which I might ever have mercy."

"Ha! fair friend," says the worthy man, "now tell me how you are named."

And he said to him: "Perceval, lord."

At this word the worthy man, who has recognized the name, sighs and says:

"Brother, much has a sin harmed you of which you do not know a word: that was the grief that your mother had of you when you departed from her; for she fell to the ground in a faint at the head of the bridge before the portal, and of this grief she died. Because of the sin that you have of this, it befell you that you did not ask of the lance nor of the grail, and there befell you many an ill for that, nor would you have lasted so long if she had not commended you to the Lord God, this know you. But her prayer had such virtue that God for her sake looked upon you and protected you from death and prison. Sin cut your language when you saw straight before you the iron which was never staunched of bleeding, and you did not inquire the reason of it. And when you did not learn of the grail whom one serves with it, you had foolish sense: he whom they serve with it is my brother;

my sister and his was your mother, and of the rich Fisher I believe that he is son to that King who has himself served with the grail. But do not believe that he has pike nor lampreys nor salmon; with a single host, which is carried to him in this grail, the holy man sustains and comforts his life. So holy a thing is the grail, and he is so spiritual that to his life nothing more is needed than the host which comes in the grail. Fifteen years has he been thus so that he has not come forth out of the room where you saw the grail enter. Now I wish to enjoin you and give you penance for your sin."

"Fair uncle, thus I wish it," says Perceval, "with very good heart. Since my mother was your sister indeed ought you to call me nephew, and I you uncle and love you better."

"True it is, fair nephew, but now hear: if pity of your soul seizes you, if you have repentance in you, and go in penitence to the minster before you go into another place each day, you will have benefit from it. Do not fail for any dispute if you are in a place where there is minster, chapel, or parish, go there when the bell sounds or before, if you have risen: never will you be grieved by this, rather will your soul be much advanced by it. And if the Mass has begun it will be so much better to be there; stay there until the priest has said everything and sung everything. If it comes to your will, you will be able to rise in worth, and you will have honor and paradise. Believe God, love God, adore God, honor a good man and good woman, get up to meet the priest; this is a service which troubles little, and God loves it in truth because it comes from humility. If a maiden seeks aid of you, help her, for it will be better for you, or a widow or orphan, that alms will be perfect; help them, thus will you do well. Take care that you leave it not off for anything—this I wish that you do for your sins—if you wish to have again all your graces just as you used to have them. Now tell me if you are willing to do it."

"Yes," says he, "very willingly."

"Now I pray you that you remain herein two entire days with me and that in penitence you take such meat as is mine."

Perceval grants it. The hermit counsels him a prayer in his ear, and repeated it until he knew it; and in that prayer there were many of the names of our Lord, for the greatest were there that mouth of man should not utter, if he name them not for fear of death. When he had taught him the prayer he forbade him that in any wise he should say it without great peril.

"I shall not do it, lord," says he.

Thus he remained and heard the service and rejoiced much. After the service he adored the Cross and wept for his sins and repented heavily, and was thus quite peaceful. That night he had to eat that which pleased the hermit; but there was in it only herbs, chervil, lettuce and cress, and there was bread of barley and oats and clear spring water; and his horse had straw and a full basin of barley, and a stable such as he should have: he was cared for as he needed.

Thus Perceval recognized that God on Friday received death and was crucified; at Easter Perceval received communion very worthily.

Of Perceval more at length the tale does not speak here, rather you will have heard much more spoken of my lord Gauvain before you hear me tell anything of him.

Further Adventures of Gauvain

MY lord Gauvain wandered so much after he escaped from the tower where the people attacked him, that between tierce and midday he came wandering toward a hill, and he saw a tall and large oak, very well leafed to give shade. On the oak he saw a shield hanging and beside it a straight lance. He hurried to move toward the oak until he saw beside it a small Norse palfrey, and it came to him as a great marvel; for they are not similar things, and, it seems to him, arms and palfrey do not occur together. If the palfrey had been a charger, then he might believe that some vassal, who for his honor and his worth might be going through the country, had mounted that hill. At once he looked beneath the oak and saw sitting there a maiden who would have seemed very beautiful to him if she had joy and gladness; but she had her fingers fixed in her tresses to pull her hair, and she was doing her best to make lament: she was making lament for a knight whom she kissed very often on the eyes, the forehead, and the mouth. When my lord Gauvain approached her, and saw the wounded knight, who had his face torn and had a very grievous sword wound in the middle of his head, and on both parts the blood ran down the sides in streams. The knight had fainted often from the pain that he had had, until finally he rested. When my lord Gauvain came there, he did

Li Contes del Graal, lines 6519-7223.

not know if he were dead or alive, and said: "Fair one, what does it seem to you of the knight whom you hold?"

And she said: "You can see that there is great peril in his wounds, for he would die of the least."

And he said to her: "My sweet friend, wake him, may it not grieve you; for I wish to ask him news of the affairs of this land."

"Lord, I would not wake him," says the maiden, "rather would I let myself be cut to pieces alive, for never did I hold any man so dear, nor will I as long as I live. I should be very foolish and wretched when I see that he is sleeping and resting, if I did anything for which he might complain of me."

"And I shall wake him, by faith, my wish," says my lord Gauvain.

Then he turns toward him the grip of his lance and touches him on the spur with it; it does not trouble the knight, for he shook his spur so softly that he did him no harm, rather he thanked him for it and said:

"Lord, I give you five hundred thanks when you have struck me and awakened me so debonairly that I am in no way harmed by it. But for yourself I pray you that you do not go forward from here, for you would do a very foolish thing. Remain, if you believe my advice."

"Remain, lord? And why should I?"

"I shall tell you," says he, "by faith, if you are willing to hear it: no knight was ever able to come from there who went there by field or way; for it is the bourn of Galvoie. Never can a knight pass there who can ever return again, nor has any yet returned from it except me, who am treated so evilly that I shall not live, as I believe, until tonight, for I found a worthy and bold and strong and fierce knight; never did I find so valiant a one nor did I try myself against such a strong one. For this I advise you it is better to go away than to go down from this hill."

"By faith," says my lord Gauvain, "that turning back would be villainous. I did not come to turn back. I should be blamed for too ugly recreancy, when I have now learned the way, if I turned back from here. I shall go far enough to know and see why no one can return from there."

"I see well that it must be done," says the injured knight; "you will go there, for you wish greatly to increase and raise your repute. But if it would not grieve you, I should very willingly pray you, if God send you the honor that never a knight has had at any time, nor do I think that it may ever happen that anyone may have it, neither you nor another by any plea, that you return this way, and that you will see, by your mercy, if I am alive or dead or whether I am better or worse. If I am dead, by charity and by the Holy Trinity I pray you of this maiden that you take care of her, that she may not have shame or discomfort. And may it please you to do this for this reason, that God never made or wished to make a nobler or more debonair, more courteous, more educated. Now it seems to me that she is very afflicted because of me, and she is not wrong, for she sees me very near death."

My lord Gauvain grants him, if hindrance does not master him either of prison or other annoyance, that he will come back by him and will give the maiden such good counsel as he will be able. Thus he leaves them and goes on his way over plains and through forests; he does not stop until he saw a very strong castle, which on one side had a very large seaport and anchorage. The castle, which was very noble, was worth little less than Pavia. On the other side was the vineyard and the great and goodly wood, which was very fair and well placed, and the river great beneath, which girded all the walls and had its course to the sea. Thus the castle and the town were fortified all around. My lord Gauvain entered into the castle over a bridge. And when he had come up, in the strongest part of the whole castle beneath an elm in a meadow he found a maiden alone, who was admiring her face and her throat, which was whiter than snow. Of a narrow circlet of goldwork she had made a crown around her head. My lord Gauvain spurs toward the maiden at an amble and she cries to him:

"Moderation, moderation! lord, now gently, for you come very foolishly! It is not fitting for you to hasten so to waste your amble. He is a fool who hurries for nothing."

"May God bless you, maiden!" says my lord Gauvain. "Now tell me, fair friend, of what you were thinking, who so quickly have reminded me of moderation, and do not know why?"

"Yes, I do, knight, by my faith, for I know well what you are thinking."

"And what?" says he.

"You wish to take me and carry me down from here on the neck of your horse."

"You have spoken truly, damsel."

"I knew it well," says she, "God's curse on him who thought it! Take care that you never think that you may put me on your horse. I am not one of those foolish Breton girls with whom those knights disport themselves who carry them away on their horses when they go on knightly adventure; but you will not carry me away. Nevertheless, if you dared, you could carry me away with you: if you were willing to trouble yourself enough to go bring me my palfrey from that garden, I should go with you until evil fortune and sorrow and grief and shame and ill luck came to you in my company."

"And will the palfrey be led hence, fair friend, except through risk?" asks he.

"To my knowledge, no, vassal," says the damsel.

"Ha! damsel, where will my horse remain, if I pass there? For he could not pass there by that plank that I see."

"No, knight: hand him over to me, and pass across on foot. I shall keep the horse for you as long as I can hold him. But hasten to return, for then I could not do more about it, if he did not want to stand in peace, or if he were taken from me by force, before you had returned."

"You have said," said he, "the truth. If he is taken from you, be quits of it, and if he escapes from you, likewise; for you will never hear me say else."

Thus he hands it over to her and goes away, and thinks that he will carry all his arms with him, for if he finds in the garden anyone who wishes to deny and forbid the palfrey that he may not go take it, there will be noise and strife rather than he bring it not away on his return.

At once he had passed over the plank and finds many people assembled, who look at him marveling and say:

"May a hundred devils burn you, maiden, who have done so much evil! May your body have evil adventure; for never did you hold worthy man dear; you have caused the head of many a worthy man to be cut off, for which there is very great grief. Knight, you who wish to lead away the palfrey, why don't you know the ills that will still come to you from this, if you touch him with your hand! Ha! knight, why do you approach him? For truly you would never approach him, if you knew the great shames and the great ills and the great pains which will come to you if you lead him away."

Thus every man and woman spoke because they wished to warn my lord Gauvain not to go for the palfrey, but to turn back. He listens to them and hears well, but for this he is not willing to leave off anything, but goes away greeting the throngs, and they all, men and women, return his greetings so that it seems that they all together have very great anguish and great distress. And my lord Gauvain moves toward the palfrey and extends his hand, and he wished to take it by the rein, for bridle and saddle were not lacking. But a very tall knight was sitting beneath a verdant olive tree, and said:

"Knight, for nothing have you come for the palfrey. Now don't stretch out a finger toward it, for you would be acting from great pride. Nevertheless I do not wish to contradict or forbid you, if you have great desire to take it; but I advise you to go away, for elsewhere than here, if you seize it, you will find too great forbiddance in it."

"I shall not give it up for that, fair lord," says my lord Gauvain, "for the maiden who is admiring herself beneath that elm sends me for it. If I did not now lead it to her, what should I have come to seek? I should be shamed on earth as recreant and without honor."

"You will be ill treated for it, fair brother," says the tall knight, "for by God the sovereign Father, to whom I should like to yield up my soul, never did a knight dare to take it, as you wish to take it, to whom there did not happen such great grief that he had his head cut off for it. Thus I fear it may befall you. And if I have forbidden it to you, I have intended no evil by that; for if you wish, you will lead it away. Never for me will you leave it, nor for any man whom you see herein, but you will hold very evil ways, if you dare take it out of here. I do not advise you to undertake it, for you would lose your head for it."

My lord Gauvain does not stop there either little or much after this word; he makes the palfrey, which had a head on one side black and on the other white, pass the plank before him, which knew very well how to pass it for it had often passed it, and was well trained and taught to do it. And my lord Gauvain took it by the rein, which was of silk, and comes straightway to the elm where the maiden was admiring herself, who had let her mantle and her wimple fall to the ground in order that her face and her body might be seen freely. My lord Gauvain delivers to her the palfrey together with its saddle and says: "Now here, come, maiden, and I shall aid you to mount."

"May God never let you tell," says the maiden, "in any place where you may come, that you have held me in your arms: if you had held anything which was on me, with your bare hand, or handled or felt it, I should believe I was shamed. It would be too unfortunate for me if it were told or known that you had touched my flesh; I should rather right on the spot, I dare well to say it, have hide and flesh cut to the bone. Leave rather the palfrey to me; for I shall indeed mount by myself. I do not wish any of your aid, and may God give me this day to see you what I think. Great joy will I then have until night. Go wherever you wish, for you will not touch my body or my clothes more closely; but I shall always go after you until through me there shall have happened to you some great discomfiture of shame and misfortune, and I am quite sure that I shall cause you to be mistreated, nor can you fail in that, even to death."

My lord Gauvain hears everything that the haughty damsel says to him, without ever sounding a word to her, except that he gives her her palfrey, and she lets him have his horse. And my lord Gauvain stoops down, who wished to lift her mantle from the ground to dress her.

The damsel, who was not slow or cowardly at saying shame to a knight, looks at him:

"Vassal," says she, "how does my mantle or my wimple concern you? By God, I am not so simple as you believe by half: I have truly no desire that you undertake to serve me, for you do not have clean hands to handle a thing that I wear or that I put on my head. Are you to grasp anything that touches my eyes or my mouth or my brow or my face? Never may God do me honor, if I have in any guise a desire to take your service."

Thus the maiden mounted, and has tied and dressed her garments and said: "Knight, now go wherever you wish to go, and I shall follow you straight way until I see you shamed because of me, and it will be today, if it please God."

My lord Gauvain keeps quiet, without ever answering her a word. Quite abashed he mounts, and they go away, and he turns, his head lowered, toward the oak where he had left the maiden and the knight, who had great need of a physician for the wounds that he had. My lord Gauvain knew more than any man how to cure a wound; he sees an herb in a hedge very good to take away grief of wound, and he goes to gather it. He collected the herb, and goes until he found the maiden uttering her grief beneath the oak. And she told him as soon as she saw him:

"Fair dear lord, now I believe that this knight is dead, for he neither hears nor heeds any more."

My lord Gauvain dismounts and finds that his pulse was very strong and that his mouth and his cheek were not too cold.

"This knight," says he, "maiden, is alive, be quite certain of it, for he has good pulse and good breath; and if he does not have a mortal wound, I bring him such an herb that will, I believe, help him much and will take

away a part of the pains from his wounds as soon as he
has felt it; for no one knows how to put on a wound a
better, thus says the letter, which testifies that it has
such force, that if anyone should place it on the bark of a
tree that was stricken, provided it was not completely
dry, its root would take hold again and the tree would
become such that it could leaf and flower. Your friend,
my damsel, would have no further care about dying, if
anyone had put this herb on his wounds and bound it
well; but a fine wimple would be needed to make a band."

"I shall hand over to you right now," says she to
whom it is no grief, "this one from off my head, for I
have brought no other here."

She took from her head the wimple, which was very
delicate and white. My lord Gauvain cuts it; for thus
he had to do, and he binds all his wounds with the herb
that he was holding. The maiden helps him as best she
knows how and can. My lord Gauvain does not move
until the knight sighs and speaks and says:

"God look upon him who has restored my speech,
for I have had great fear of dying without confession.
The devils in procession had already come to seek my
soul. Before my body be put in earth, I should very
much like to be confessed. I know a chaplain near here,
if I had something to mount on, to whom I should go
say and tell my sins in confession, and should take communion: never should I fear death, after I had taken
communion and had made my confession. But now do
me a service, if it does not trouble you: give me that
squire's nag which is coming there at a trot."

When my lord Gauvain hears him, he turns around
and sees coming a disagreeable squire. And what was he?
I shall tell you: his hair was mixed-colored and red,
stiff and standing erect as a pig which is bristling, and his

eyebrows were the same; for they covered all his face and nose as far as his whiskers, which were twisted and long; his mouth was split and his beard wide, forked and then curled back, and his neck short and his chest high. My lord Gauvain wishes to go to meet him to see if he could have the nag, but first he says to the knight:

"Lord, if the Lord God help me, I do not know who the squire is: I would rather give you seven chargers, if I had them here at my right hand, than his nag, such as it can be."

"Lord," says he, "now know well that he goes seeking nothing except your harm, if he can."

My lord Gauvain moves to meet the squire who was coming, and asks him where he was going.

He, who was not debonair, said to him: "Vassal, what have you to do with where I am going or whence I come, whatever way I may hold? May your body have evil adventure!"

My lord Gauvain rightly pays him at once his desert, for he strikes him with open palm while he had his arm ready and great desire to strike him, so that he knocks him over and empties the saddle. When he thinks to get up, he staggers and falls down again and faints seven times or more in less space, without any exaggeration, than a fir lance takes up. And when he had gotten up again, he said: "Vassal, you struck me."

"Truly," says he, "I struck you, but I have scarcely damaged you; still I regret that I struck you, if God see me; but you said great folly to me."

"Still I shall not leave off without telling you what desert you shall have for it: You will for that lose the hand and the arm with which you have given me the blow, for it will never be pardoned you."

While this happened, his heart, which was very weak,

came back to the wounded knight, and he said to my lord
Gauvain:

"Leave that squire, fair lord; for you will never hear
him say anything in which you are to have honor. Leave
him, and you will do wisely, but bring me his nag and
take this maiden whom you see here beside me and bridle
her palfrey; then aid her to mount, for I do not wish
to be here any longer, rather shall I mount, if ever I
can, on the nag and then I shall seek where I may con-
fess myself, for I do not wish to cease to be until I be
anointed and confessed and communed."

At once my lord Gauvain takes the nag and hands
it over to the knight, whose sight was relighted and returned, and he saw my lord Gauvain: then for the first
time he recognized him. And my lord Gauvain took the
maiden, and put her on the Norse palfrey debonairly and
courteously. While he seated her on it, the knight
took his horse and mounted on it, and began to dash from
here to there, and my lord Gauvain looks at him who
was galloping over the hill and marvels at it and laughs
at it and while laughing says this to him:

"Lord knight, by my faith, it is great folly that I
see when you prance my horse. Dismount, and hand him
over to me, for you could quickly harm yourself and make
your wounds burst open."

And he answers: "Gauvain, be quiet, take the nag,
and you will do wisely, for you have lost the horse: I
have tried him out to my need, and I shall lead him away
as mine."

"Ha! I came here for your good, and you would
do me such evil? Do not lead away my horse, for you
would do treason."

"Gauvain, by such a mistake, whatever were to happen
to me for it, I should like to hold your heart from your
belly in my two hands."

"Now hear I," answers Gauvain, "a proverb that is said; for it is said: 'from benefit, broken neck,' but I should like very much to know why you would like to have my heart and take my horse from me; for never do I wish to do you harm, nor did I in all my life. I did not think to have deserved this from you: never before, that I know of, did I see you."

"Yes, you have, Gauvain, you saw me there where you did me great shame: do you not remember the one to whom you did such great annoyance that he had against his will to eat with the dogs for a month, his hands bound behind his back? Know that you did very foolishly, for now you have great shame because of it."

"Are you then that Greorreas, who took the damsel by force and made your good of her? Nevertheless you knew well that in the land of King Arthur maidens are secure; the King has given them truces and guards them and conducts them, nor do I think or believe that you may hate me for this misdeed nor that you do me any evil for that, because I did it for legal justice, which is established and seated throughout all the King's land."

"Gauvain, you took justice of me, well do I remember it, and it behooves you to suffer what I shall do, for I shall lead away the Gringalet. Further I cannot now avenge myself; you must exchange it for the nag from which you knocked the squire, for other exchange you will not have."

At once Greorreas leaves him and rushes after his friend, who was going away at a great amble, and he follows her at a great pace. The evil maiden laughs and says to my lord Gauvain:

"Vassal, vassal, what will you do? Now can it indeed be said without hesitating that 'evil deceiver is not dead.' Well do I know that mine is the wrong of it to follow you, if God keep me: never will you turn in any direction that I will not follow you very gladly. And would that now the nag that you took from the squire were a mare! I should like it, know that, because you would have more shame!"

At once my lord Gauvain mounts on the trotting nag as one who could not do better. In the nag there was a very ugly beast; its neck was thin, its head large, ears wide and hanging and from old age it had such teeth that one lip of its mouth does not touch the other by two fingers; its eyes were troubled and dim, its feet cracked, its sides hard, all torn by spurs. The nag was thin and long, and had a lean crupper and a long backbone. The reins and the headpiece of the bridle were of a small cord; the saddle was without covering, for it was long since it was new. He finds the stirrups short and weak so that he does not dare fix himself in them.

"Ha! certainly, now things go well!" says the insulting maiden, "now shall I be glad and joyous to go wherever you wish! Now is it indeed reason and right that I follow you gladly a week or two whole weeks or three or a month! Now are you well equipped! Now are you sitting on a good charger, now you indeed resemble a knight who should escort a maiden! Now first do I wish to delight myself at seeing your misfortunes! Prod your horse with your spurs a little, and try him out, and don't be dismayed, for he is very spirited and nimble. I shall follow you: for it is very fitting that I shall never leave you until some shame befalls you for certain, for you will not escape it."

And he answers her: "Fair friend, you will say what is good to you; but it does not befit a damsel that she be so ill-spoken after she has passed ten years; rather she ought to be well taught and courteous and well trained."

"Knight by evil chance, I have no care for your instruction; but go and be quiet, for now you are as comfortable as I wished to see you."

Thus they ride until evening and both keep quiet.

He goes on, and she after him; but he does not know what he can do with his nag, for he can draw from it neither trot nor gallop for any effort; whether he wishes or not, he goes at a walk, for if he beats it with his spurs, he urges it into too hard a pace that so shakes his inwards that he can not suffer going at more than a walk in any manner.

The Castle of the Maidens

THUS he goes along on the nag through waste and lonely forests until he came to flat lands on a river deep and so broad that no sling of mangonel or of onager could throw across the river, nor crossbow shoot across it. On the other side of the water sat a very well built castle, very strong and very rich.

I do not wish to let myself lie about it: the castle sat on a cliff and was of such richness that never did eyes of living man see such a rich fortress; and on a native rock there was a well placed palace, which was all of dark marble. In the palace there were well five hundred open windows, all covered with ladies and damsels, who were looking at the flowering meadows and gardens before them. Most of the damsels were dressed in samite; they wore bliauts of divers colors and cloths of silk, most with beaten gold.

Thus the maidens stood at the windows and their shining heads and gentle bodies appeared there, so that they were seen there from their belts up. And the most evil thing in the world, who was leading my lord Gauvain, comes straight to the river; then she stops and dismounts from the little dappled palfrey and finds at the banks a boat, which was fastened with a key and attached to a block of stone. In the boat there was an oar, and on the stone was the key with which the boat was fastened. The damsel, who had an evil heart in her

Li Contes del Graal, lines 7224-9234.

bosom, enters the boat, and her palfrey after her, which had done the same many a time.

"Vassal," says she, "dismount and enter here after me with your horse, which is leaner than a baby chick, and unanchor this flatboat, for indeed you will enter into an evil year if you do not pass this water quickly or if you can not flee quickly."

"Ha! damsel, why?"

"You do not see what I see, knight, for you would flee very quickly, if you saw."

My lord Gauvain at once turns his head and sees a knight coming across the plain completely armed, and he asks the maiden: "Now may it not grieve you: tell me who is that one who is sitting on my horse which the traitor whom I cured of his wounds this morning took from me?"

"I shall tell you, by Saint Martin," says the maiden, "joyously. But know well truly that I should not tell it to you if I saw in it a bit of your good; but because I am sure that he is coming for your misfortune, I shall not conceal it from you. It is the nephew of Greorreas, whom he sends here after you, and I shall indeed tell you why, since you have asked me: his uncle has commanded him to follow you until he has killed you and brought him your head as a present. Therefore I advise you to dismount if you do not wish to await death; enter in here and flee from him."

"Certainly, I shall not flee from him, damsel, but rather I shall wait for him."

"Never more, truly, shall I forbid you," says the damsel, "rather I keep quiet about it; for fine spurring and fine prancing will you make indeed before the maidens there who are courtly and beautiful, leaning on those windows. Because of you the affair pleases them, and they have come there for you. Truly indeed will they

make great joy when they see you stumble. Much do
you now resemble a knight who ought to joust with another."

"Whatever it may cost me, maiden, I shall not avoid
it, but I shall go to meet him, but if I could recover my
horse, I should be very glad of it."

At once he turns away toward the plain and turns the
head of his nag toward the one who was coming spurring
across the sand. And my lord Gauvain awaits him, and
settles himself so hard in the stirrups that he breaks the
left one all around, and he abandoned the right one, and
he waits for the knight thus, because the nag never moves,
and he can not spur it enough to make it move.

"Alas!" says he, "what a bad seat a knight has on
a nag when he wishes to do feats of arms!"

Meanwhile the knight spurs toward him on the horse,
which does not limp, and gives him such a blow with his
lance that it bows and shatters through and through and
the iron remains in his shield. And my lord Gauvain
strikes him on his shield in the middle of the top and
thrusts at him so that he passes the lance through his
shield and hauberk together and knocks him down on the
fine sand; and Gauvain extends his hand, and has caught
the horse and leaps into the saddle. This fortune was
fair to him, and he had such joy in his heart that never
in all his life was he so glad of such an outcome. He
turns back to the maiden, who had entered the boat; but
he has found nothing either of the boat or of her, and
this displeased him very much when he had lost her thus
that he does not know what has become of her.

While he was thinking of the maiden, he sees coming
a small boat that a boatman was bringing, who was coming from toward the castle. And when he had come to
the port, he said:

"Lord, I bring you greetings on behalf of these

damsels, and with them they send you word that you retain not my fief: give it back to me, if you deign."

And he answers: "God bless all together the company of the damsels and then you! You will never lose anything through me in which you may claim a right. I have no care for doing you wrong; but what fief are you demanding of me?"

"Lord, you have beaten down here a knight whose charger I am to have; if you do not wish to act wrongly toward me, you are to hand over the charger to me."

And he answers: "Friend, this fief would be too grievous to me to hand over, for I should have to go back on foot."

"Ha! knight, now truly I hold you for very disloyal and these maidens whom you see consider it a very great evil when you do not hand over my fief to me; it never happened nor was it said that at this port a knight was knocked down, provided I knew it, that I did not have his horse, or if I did not have the horse, I could not fail to have the knight."

And my lord Gauvain says to him: "Friend, take the knight without contradiction and keep him."

"He is not yet so dismayed," says the boatman, "by my faith. You yourself, as I believe, would have much to do to take him, if he wished to defend himself against you. And, nevertheless, if you are worth so much, go take him and bring him to me, and you will be quit of my fief."

"Friend, if I dismount, shall I be able to trust you to keep my horse in faith?"

"Yes," says he, "surely. I shall guard him loyally, and return him to you willingly, nor shall I do wrong to you in anything as long as I am alive, well do I grant and pledge it to you."

"And I," says he, "in turn trust you on your pledge and your faith."

At once he dismounts from his horse, and commends it to him, and he takes it who says that he will keep it in faith. And my lord Gauvain goes with sword drawn toward him who needs no more trouble, for he was so wounded in the side that he had lost much blood. And my lord Gauvain passes to him.

"Lord, I do not know that I might conceal from you," says he who was very dismayed, "that I am so badly wounded that I have no need to have worse: I have lost a gallon of blood, and so I put myself at your mercy."

"Now then," says he, "get up from here."

And he gets up with some labor, and my lord Gauvain leads him to the boatman, who thanks him for him. And my lord Gauvain prays him that he tell him of a maiden, if he knows any news of her, whom he had brought there, what direction she had gone. And he said:

"Lord, don't be concerned about the maiden, wherever she may go: for maiden is she not, rather is worse than Sathenas, for she has had the heads of many knights cut off at this port. But if you were willing to believe me, today you would come to lodge in such hostel as is mine; for it would not be your well-being to remain on this bank, for this is a wild country all full of great marvels."

"Friend, when you advise me, I am willing to hold to your counsel, whatever may happen to me for it."

He does so according to the advice of the boatman, and pulls his horse after him, and enters the boat, and they go away, they have come to the other bank. The hostel of the boatman was near the water and it was such that a count might stop there, it was so very comfortable and good. The boatman leads his guest and his prisoner

there and makes over them the greatest joy that he can.
My lord Gauvain was served with everything a worthy
man needs: he had plovers and pheasants and partridges
and venison for supper, and the wines were strong and
clear, white and vermilion, new and old. The boatman
was very glad of his prisoner and of his guest. They ate
until the table was taken away, and they wash their hands
again. That night my lord Gauvain had hostel and host
to his liking, for he took very willingly the service of the
boatman and it pleased him very much. The next day,
as soon as he could see that the day appeared, he got up
as he should, for he was thus accustomed. And the boatman also, for love of him, and they were both leaning at
the windows of a small tower. My lord Gauvain looked
at the country, which was very beautiful; he saw the
forests and saw the plains and the castle on the cliff.

"Host," says he, "if it does not trouble you, I wish
to ask you and inquire: who is lord of this land and of
this castle here at hand?"

The host answers him at once: "Lord, I do not
know."

"You do not know? It is a marvel; for you have
told me that you are sergeant of the castle and you have
very great income from it, and you do not know who is
the lord of it?"

"For truth," says he, "can I tell you that I do not
know, nor did I ever know."

"Fair host, now tell me then: who defends and guards
the castle?"

"Lord, there is a very good guard there: five hundred,
bowmen as well as crossbowmen, who are always ready to
draw; if anyone tried to do anything wrong, they would
never stop drawing nor would they ever be wearied: they
are made with such craft. But I shall tell you so much

of the assembly that there is a queen, a very high lady
and rich and wise, and she is of very great peerage. The
queen with all her treasure, which was very great in
silver and gold, came to dwell in this country and has
made here such a strong manor as you can see here, and
brought with her a lady whom she loves so much that she
calls her queen and daughter. And this one has another
daughter, who does not debase her lineage, nor does it
any shame, nor do I believe that under heaven there is a
more beautiful or better educated. And the hall is very
well guarded by art and by enchantment as you will know
next, if it please you that I tell it to you: a cleric wise in
astronomy, whom the queen brought there, in that great
palace, has done such great marvels that you never heard
their equals; for a knight can not enter there who can stop
there an hour alive and healthy who is full of covetousness,
nor who has in him any evil vice of flattery or of avarice;
coward or traitor does not last there, nor treachery nor
forsworn perjury: those die there so freely that they can
not last nor live there. But there are many retainers
there from many lands who for arms serve those therein;
there are well as many as five hundred of them, some
bearded, the others not: a hundred who have neither beard
nor moustache, and a hundred others on whom beards
sprout and a hundred who shave and trim their beards each
week, and there are a hundred whiter than wool and a
hundred who are turning gray. There are ancient ladies
there who have neither husbands nor lords, but rather
have been disinherited of lands and honors in great wrong
since their husbands had died; and orphan damsels are
there with the two queens, who hold them in very great
honor. Such people come and go in the palace, and they
are waiting for a great folly which could not happen, for
they are waiting for a knight to come therein who will re-

store to the ladies their honors and will give lords to the damsels and make knights of the youths. But the sea will be all of ice before such a knight may be found who can remain in the palace; for he would have to be perfectly wise and generous, without covetousness, handsome and noble, bold and loyal, without villainy and without any evil; if such a one could come here, he could hold the palace, he could restore their lands to the ladies, he would make peace of many wars, he would marry the maidens and would dub the youths and would take away completely the enchantments from the palace."

This news pleased my lord Gauvain and was very fair to him.

"Host," says he, "let us go down and have my arms and horse handed over to me without delay; for I do not wish to wait here longer, rather shall I go away."

"Lord, in what direction? Now stay, if God keep you, today and tomorrow and even longer."

"Host, it will not be now, although blessed be your hostel! But I shall go, so help me God, to see those ladies up there and the marvels which are there."

"Be quiet, lord! If it please God, you will not do this folly, but believe me, and remain."

"Be quiet, host! You hold me for recreant and for coward. May God never more have a share in my soul if I believe any counsel about it."

"By faith, lord, and I shall be silent about it, for it would be wasted effort. When the going is so agreeable to you, you will go there, which troubles me much, and I must conduct you there; for other escort, know this well, would avail you nothing. But I wish to have a gift from you."

"Host, what gift? I wish to know it."

"First you will have granted it to me."

"Fair host, I shall do your will, provided there is no shame in it."

Then he commands that his charger be drawn out of the stable for him completely ready for riding, and he has asked for his arms, and they are brought to him. He arms himself and mounts, and turns away. And the boatman, who wishes to guide him in faith there where he is going against his will, makes himself ready to mount on his palfrey. They go until at the foot of the steps before the palace they find, sitting all alone on a bundle of rushes, a cripple who had a crutch of silver; it was well gilded with niello, and here and there was banded with gold and precious stones. The cripple's hands were not idle, for he held a small knife and was intent on smoothing a stick of ash. The cripple addresses no word to those who go in front of him, nor have they said any word to him. And the boatman pulls my lord Gauvain to him and says:

"Lord, what do you think of this cripple?"

"His crutch is not of poplar wood," says my lord Gauvain, "by faith, for what I see pleases me well."

"In the name of God," says the boatman, "he is rich, the cripple, with very great and beautiful income. You might hear such news that might annoy you very much, if it were not for the fact that I bear you company and guide you."

Thus they both pass along until they have come to the palace, whose entry was very high and the doors rich and beautiful; for all the hinges and the bolts were of fine gold, witness the story. One of the doors was of ivory well carved above; the other door was of ebony likewise worked above, and each was illuminated with gold and stones of virtue. The pavement of the palace was green and vermilion, indigo and greenish blue, of all colors it was diversified, very well worked and polished. In the middle of the palace was a bed in which there was nothing of wood; there was nothing which was not of gold except only the cords which were all of silver.

Of the bed I make no fable, for on each one of the cord knots there was a bell hung. On the bed there was spread a great cover of samite; on each of the posts of the bed there was a carbuncle fastened, which gave off as great light as four well-lighted candles. The bed was placed on sculptured dogs which showed much ill-humor by their jaws, and the dogs on four wheels so swift and so moving that with a single finger everywhere therein the bed might go from end to the other, if anyone should push it. Such was the bed, if anyone should tell the truth of it, that never for king nor for count was such a one made nor will ever be made. And all the palace was covered with tapestries and I wish that one believe me that there was nothing in it of chalk: the inner walls were of marble; in the upper edge there were panes so clear, if anyone should take notice of them, that through the glass he might see all those who entered the palace and passed through the door. The glass was painted in colors of the richest and of the best that anyone knows how to devise or make; but I do not wish now to retrace or devise all the things. In the palace there were a good four hundred windows closed and a hundred open. My lord Gauvain very surely went looking at the palace both up and down and here and there. When he had looked everywhere, he called the boatman and said:

"Fair host, I see herein nothing for which this palace causes such dread that anyone should not indeed enter it. Now say: what did you intend when you so strongly forbade me to come here to see? I wish to sit down on that bed and rest just a little, for never did I see so rich a bed."

"Ha! fair lord, God keep you from going near it;

for if you approached it, you would die the worst death by which any knight ever died."

"Host, what shall I do then?"

"What, lord? That I shall tell you, when I see you encouraged to keep your life: when you had to come here, I asked you at my hostel for a gift, but you did not know what. Now I wish to ask you for the gift that you go back to your land, and you will tell your friends and the people of your country that you have seen such a palace that you know none so rich, nor do you or any other know one."

"Then shall I say that God hates me and that I am shamed together. Nevertheless, host, it seems to me that you are saying it for my good. But I should not leave off for anything that I should not sit on the bed nor see the maidens that yesterday evening I saw leaning on the windows which are here."

He who draws back in order to flee better answers him:

"You will see none of the maidens of whom you are speaking. But go back again just as you came in here; for of seeing there is nothing to your profit for anything, and they indeed see you right now through the glass windows, the maidens and the queens and the ladies, so keep me God, who are in the rooms on the other side."

"By faith," says my lord Gauvain, "I shall sit down on the bed at least, if I do not see the maidens, for I do not think or believe that such a bed should be made if not so that one might lie in it, either gentle man or high lady. And I shall go sit on it, by my soul, whatever may happen to me for it."

He sees that he can not hold him back, and lets the word stand, but he can not stop in the palace until he sees him sit on the bed, but holds his way and says:

"Lord, of your death I am much troubled and greatly

grieved; for no knight ever sat on that bed who did not die in it; for it is the Bed of the Marvel, where no one sleeps or slumbers, or reposes in it or sits on it who ever gets up healthy or alive. It is a very great pity about you, when you will leave your head there in pawn without repurchase and without ransom. When by love and by dispute I can not lead you from here, may God have mercy on your soul; for my heart could not suffer me to see you die."

At once he goes forth from the palace. And my lord Gauvain sat down on the bed so armed as he was, that he had his shield at his neck when he sat. And the cords throw out a cry and all the bells sound so that they stun the whole palace, and all the windows open and the marvels are uncovered and the enchantments appear, so that quarrels and arrows flew in through the windows, and more than five hundred of them struck my lord Gauvain on the shield; but he did not know who had struck him. The enchantment was such that no man could see from what part the bolts came nor the archers who were shooting them. And this can you well understand that there was great thunder at the release of the crossbows and bows and my lord Gauvain would not wish to be there at that hour for a thousand marks. But the windows closed again without delay, for no one pushed. And my lord Gauvain took out the quarrels which had struck in his shield, and had so wounded him in several places in his body that the blood rushed forth. Before he had drawn them all, another dispute had broken upon him, for a villein struck a door with a staff, and the door opened and a very marvelous and strong and fierce and hungry lion leaps through the door from a chamber and assails my lord Gauvain with great ferocity and great anger, and it sinks its talons in his shield just as in wax and knocks it down so that it makes him come to his knees. But he leaps up at once and draws his good sword from its scabbard and strikes so that he has cut off its head and both feet. Then my lord Gauvain was glad; for the feet remained hung by the nails on his shield so that one appeared inside and the other hanging outside. When he had slain the lion, and had sat down again on the bed, his host with joyous face came back into the palace at once, and found him sitting on the bed and said:

"Lord, I grant you that you no longer have any fear. Take away all your armor; for the marvels of the palace have been removed, for all days more, by you who have come here; and you will be served and honored by the young and by the white-haired herein, for which God be adored!"

At once youths come in crowds, with bodies very well dressed in tunics, and they all put themselves on their knees and say:

"Fair dear sweet lord, we present you our services as to that one whom we have long awaited and desired; for you have too long delayed for our advantage, it seems to us."

Straightway one of them has taken him, and begins to disarm him, and the others go to stable his horse which was outside. And while he was disarming himself, a maiden entered therein who was beautiful and capable, on her head a circlet of gold; her hair was yellow as much as gold or more. Her face was white and over the white Nature had illuminated it with a vermilion and pure color; the maiden was very adroit, beautiful and well made, long and straight. After her came other maidens rather gentle and beautiful; and one youth came there all alone, who held to his neck a robe and tunic, mantle and surcoat; there was a piece of ermine in the mantle and sable black as a mulberry, and the covering on top was of vermilion scarlet. My lord Gauvain marvels at the maidens whom he sees coming, nor can he hold himself from leaping to his feet to meet them, and he says: "Maidens, welcome!"

The first bows to him and says: "My lady the queen, fair dear lord, sends greetings to you and to all these maidens commands that they hold you for their right lord and that they all come to serve you. As the very first, I promise you my service without pretense, and these maidens who come here all hold you for their lord, for they had much longed for you and are joyous when they see you the best of all worthy men. Lord, that is all, except that we are ready to serve you."

At this word all kneeled and bow to him as those who destine themselves to serve and honor him. He without delay makes them rise and then sit; for much are they pleasing to him to see, partly because they are beautiful and more because they make of him their prince and their lord. Joy he has, for never did he have greater, from the honor that God has done him. Then the maiden came forward and said:

"My lady sends you this robe to put on before she sees you, since she believes, as one who is not void of courtesy or of sense, that you have great travail and great suffering and great trouble: but put it on, and try it whether it is good to your measure; for after the heat those who are wise guard themselves from the cold, for one has blood trouble and freezes from it. For this reason my lady the queen sends you a robe of ermine, so that the cold may not do you harm; for just as water becomes ice, the blood congeals and freezes together after the heat when a man trembles."

My lord Gauvain answers as the most courteous in the world: "May that Lord in whom no good is lacking save my lady the queen, and you as the well speaking and the courteous and the capable! The lady is, this I believe, very wise when her messengers are so courteous: she knows well what is needed by and suited to a knight, when she, by her mercy, sends me here a robe to put on; thank her very much for it for me."

"So shall I do willingly, I grant you," says the maiden, "and you can meanwhile dress and look at the condition of this country through these windows, and you can, if it pleases you, mount on that tower to look at forests and plains and rivers until I have returned."

At once the maiden turns away. My lord Gauvain adorns himself with the robe, which was very rich, and he fastens his collar with a clasp which hung at the neck opening; then he has a desire to go see the things which are on the tower. Both he and his host go there, and they mount by a winding stair which was beside the vaulted palace until they came to the top of the tower, and they see the country around more beautiful than one could say. My lord Gauvain looks all around at the river and the flat lands and the forests full of beasts, and looked from them to his host and said to him: "Host, by God, it pleases me much to stay here to go hunting and shooting arrows in these forests before us."

"Lord," says the boatman, "of this can you well keep silent; for I have often heard it related that he whom God would love so much that he would be called master and lord and defender herein, it is established and vowed that never more would he go forth from these lodgings, were it wrong or right. Therefore it does not behoove you to speak of hunting or of pulling the bow; for herein have you your abode, never will you go forth on any day."

"Host," says he, "be quiet about it. You would

throw me out of my senses, if I heard you say more. So help me God, I could not live in here for seven days any more than for seven score years for the reason that I might not go forth every time that I wished."

At once he went down again and re-entered the palace, very angry and very pensive, and he sat down on the bed with very grieving and mournful face until the maiden returns who had been there before. When my lord Gauvain sees her, he stood up to meet her, just as angered as he was, and greeted her at once. And she saw that he had changed his speech and his countenance, and it seemed from his appearance that he was angered by something; but she does not dare to give any sign of it but says: "Lord, when it will please you, my lady will come to see you. But the meal is prepared, and you will eat, if you wish, either down here or up there."

My lord Gauvain answers: "Fair one, I have no care for eating. May my body have evil fortune if I eat or have joy before I hear news over which I may rejoice, for I have great need to hear such."

The maiden very dismayed turned away at once, and the queen calls her to her and asks her:

"What news? Fair niece," says the queen, "in what state and thought have you found the good lord whom God has given us herein?"

"Ha! honored lady queen, I am dead of grief and heart-rent over the noble lord, the debonair, from whom one can not draw a word which is not of wrath or anger; and I do not know how to tell you the why; for he has not told me, nor do I know, nor did I dare ask him. But I can indeed tell you of him that the first time today I found him so well mannered, so well spoken and taught, that one could not be satiated at hearing his words or seeing his handsome face: now he is so soon of a different

manner that he would like to be dead, this I think, for he
hears nothing that does not trouble him."

"Niece, now don't be dismayed, for he will be quickly
calmed as soon as he sees me: never will he have such
great ire in his heart that I shall not quickly have put
it out and put great joy in place of ire."

Then the queen moved, and came into the palace,
and the other queen with her, whom the going pleased
greatly, and they led after them well five hundred damsels
and as many youths at least. As soon as my lord Gauvain
saw the queen who was coming and who held the other
by the hand, his heart tells him and divines that it was
that queen of whom he had heard spoken; but he could
easily divine it when he saw the white tresses, which hung
over her hips, and she was dressed in a white diapered
silk with flowers of gold, of minute work. When my
lord Gauvain looks at her, he does not delay in going to
meet her, and greets her and she him, and she said to
him:

"Lord, I am lady after you in this palace: I leave
you the lordship of it, for you have very well disputed
the possession of it. But are you of the household of King
Arthur?"

"Lady, I am, truly."

"And are you, I wish to know it, of the knights of
the watch who have done many a prowess?"

"No, lady."

"Well do I believe you. And are you, tell me, of
those of the Round Table, who are the most prized in the
world?"

"Lady," says he, "I should not dare to say that I
am of the most prized, nor do I make myself of the
best, nor do I think to be of the worst."

And she answers him: "Fair lord, great courtesy

do I hear you say who do not put on yourself the prize of the best nor the blame of the worst. But now tell me of King Lot: of his wife how many sons did he have?"

"Lady, four."

"Now name them to me!"

"Lady, Gauvain is the eldest, and the second is Agrevain the Proud with the hard hands; Gaheriez and Guerehes are the names of the other two after them."

And the Queen says again to him: "Lord, if the Lord God help me, thus are they named, it seems to me. Now might it please God that they were all here together with you! Now tell me: do you know King Uriien?"

"Yes, lady."

"And has he no son at the court?"

"Lady, yes, two of great renown: one is named my lord Yvain, the courteous, the well trained; I am more cheered all day long when I can see him in the morning, so wise and so courteous do I find him. And the other is also named Yvain, who is not his brother-german; for this they call him the Bastard, and he surpasses all the knights who take battle with him. Both these at the court are very wise, very worthy, and very courteous."

"Fair lord," says she, "how is King Arthur living now?"

"Better than he ever did before, healthier, lighter, and stronger."

"By faith, lord, that is not wrong, for he is a child, is King Arthur: if he is a hundred years old, he isn't any more, nor can he be more. But further I wish to know of you, that you tell me solely of the state and of the manner of life of the Queen, if it trouble you not."

"Lady, truly, she is so courteous and so beautiful and so wise that God made no religion nor language in which one might find so wise a lady. Since God formed the first woman from the rib of Adam, there has been no lady so renowned, and she ought indeed to be so: just as the wise master teaches the little children, so my lady the Queen teaches and gives lessons to all the world, for from her all good descends and comes and moves. No one can depart from my lady who may go away disconsolate; for she knows well what each one is worth and what one ought to do for each one in order that she may please him. No man does good or honor to whom my lady has not taught it, nor may anyone ever be so ill-humored that he may part from my lady in anger."

"Nor will you do so, lord, from me."

"Lady," says he, "well do I believe you, for before I saw you, I was so afflicted and grieving that I cared not what I did. Now I am so glad and joyous that I could not be more so."

"Lord, by God who caused me to be born," says the Queen with the white tresses, "your happiness will yet double and your joy will increase at once, nor will they ever fail you more. And when you are joyous and glad, the food is made ready for you, and you will eat, when you please, in whatever place it will suit you: if it please you, you will eat up here, and if it please you, you will come into the chambers down there to eat."

"Lady, I do not wish to change this palace for any chamber, for I am told that never did a knight eat or sit in it."

"No, lord, who came out of it again alive, or who remained alive in it an hour or a half."

"Lady, then shall I eat in it, if you give me leave to do so."

"I give it to you, lord, gladly, and you will be the very first knight who has eaten in it."

At once the Queen goes away, and leaves him well a hundred and fifty of the most beautiful, of her maidens who ate in the palace beside him, and served him and

cajoled him with whatever came to his liking. More than
a hundred valets served him at the meal, some of whom
were all white, and the others were turning gray, and
others not; the others had neither beard nor whiskers,
and, of those, two were on their knees before him, and
one of them served him by cutting his meat, and the
other in pouring wine.

My lord Gauvain made his host eat side by side with
him. And the meal was not short, for it lasted longer
than one of the days around Nativity lasts; for it was
close and dark night, and there were many great torches
burned there before the meal was finished. During the
meal there were many words, and there were many
dances and carols after eating, before they went to bed;
all wearied themselves at making joy for their lord whom
they hold very dear. And when he wished to go to bed,
he lay down in the Bed of the Marvel. One of the maidens
put a pillow under his ear, which made him sleep at
ease. And the next day at awakening they had made
ready for him a robe of ermine and samite. The boatman
came before his bed in the morning, and had him get up
and dress and wash his hands. At his getting up was
Clarissanz, the worthy, the beautiful, the goodly, the wise,
the well-spoken girl. Then she entered the chamber
and kneels before the queen, who asks her and hugs her:

"Niece, faith that you owe me, is your lord up yet?"

"Yes, lady, a long time ago."

"And where is he, my fair niece?"

"Lady, he went up on the tower, and I do not know
if he came down afterward."

"Niece, I wish to go to him, and, if it please God,
never more today shall I have anything but good and
joy and gladness."

At once the queen stands up, for she has a desire
to go to him. She goes until she finds him up at the

windows of a tower where he was looking at a maiden,
and saw an armed knight who was coming down a meadow
there where it was within his view.   Meanwhile behold
on the other side the two queens side by side; they have
found my lord Gauvain and his host at two windows.

"Lord, may you have gotten up well!" say both the
queens, "may this day be glad and joyous for you! May
that glorious Father who made His daughter His mother
give you that!"

"Lady, may He who sent on earth His Son to exalt
Christianity give you great joy!   But if you will, come to
this window and tell me: who can a maiden be who is coming here, and has with her a knight who bears a quartered
shield?"

"I shall tell you very willingly," says the lady who
look at them, "she is the one, whom may evil fire burn,
who brought you here yesterday evening!   But do not
concern yourself about her, for she is too perfidious and
villainous.   I pray you not to worry about the knight
whom she is bringing; for he is, know it well without fail,
courageous above all knights.   His battle is no play, for
in my sight he has conquered and killed many a knight
at this port."

"Lady," says he, "I wish to go speak to the damsel,
if you give me leave to do so."

"Lord, may it not please God that I give you leave
for your harm!   Let that troublesome damsel go about
her business.   Never, if it please God, will you go out
of your palace for such a useless matter.   You ought never
to go out of it again, if you do not wish to do us wrong."

"Ha! debonair queen, now have you much dismayed
me: I shall hold myself badly paid with the palace,
if I did not go out of it.   May it not please God that I
should be thus long a prisoner in it!"

"Ha! lady," says the boatman, "let him do all his

own good. Do not hold him against his will, for he could die of grief for it."

"I shall let him go out," says the queen, "by covenant that, if God defend him from death, he will come back again tonight."

"Lady," says he, "let it not trouble you, for I shall return, if I am able. But one gift I ask and beg of you, if it please you and you command, that you do not ask my name before seven days, if it grieve you not."

"And I, lord, since it suits you, shall suffer it," says the queen, "for I do not wish to have your hatred, and it might be the first thing that I might have prayed you, that you should tell me your name, if you had not forbidden me."

Thus they go down from the tower, and servants come, and give him his arms to arm his body, and they have brought him his horse, and he mounts it fully armed, and has gone to the port, and the boatman with him, and they both enter a boat and rowed so briskly that they have come to the other bank, and my lord Gauvain goes out of it. And the other knight says to the maiden without mercy:

"Friend, tell me, do you know this knight who comes here armed against us?"

"No, but I know well that he is the one who yesterday brought me to these parts."

And he answers: "If God keep me, I was going seeking no other. I have had great fear that he might have escaped me; for knight born of mother never passed the ports of Galvoie, if it so happens that I see him and find him before me, who can ever boast elsewhere that he has come from this country. This one is indeed taken and held as soon as God lets me see him."

At once the knight rushes forward without defiance

and without threat; he spurs his horse, sets his shield on his arm. And my lord Gauvain directs himself toward him, and strikes him so that he wounds him very greatly in the arm and in the side; but he was not wounded to death, for the hauberk held so well that the iron could not pass through it, except that he puts a full finger of the very point of the lance in his body, and bears him to earth. He gets up, and sees his blood, which grieves him much; for from his arm and from his side it was flowing over his white hauberk, and it runs down upon his sword. But he was wearied in little time so that he could not stand, but rather he had to come to mercy. My lord Gauvain takes his pledge and then hands him over to the boatman who was waiting for him. And the evil maiden had dismounted from her palfrey. He comes to her, and greets her and says:

"Mount again, fair friend. I shall not leave you here, rather shall lead you with me across that water where I am to pass."

"Hai!" says she, "knight, you act now very haughty and fierce. You would have battle enough, if my friend had not been wearied from old wounds that he has had. Your boasting would fall away, you would not carry on so much big talk, you would be more mute than a post in a corner. But now admit the truth to me: do you believe you are worth more because you have beaten him down? It often happens, as you know well, that the weak beats down the strong. But if you left this port and came together with me toward that tree and did one thing that my friend, whom you have put in the boat, did for me when I wished, then truly would I bear witness that you were worth better than he, nor would I any longer hold you vile."

"As for going that far, maiden," says he, "your will will be done without fail."

And she says: "May it not please God that I see you return from there!"

At once they set out on the way, she before and he afterward, and the maidens of the palace and the ladies pull their hair and scratch and tear their faces and say:

"Ha! miserable wretches, why are we any longer alive when we see going to his death and sorrow that one who was to be our lord? The evil maiden escorts him, and the hussy leads him there whence no knight returns. Alas! we are so heart-rent who were born at such a good hour, for God had sent us the one who knew all good things, the one in whom nothing was lacking, neither boldness nor other good."

Thus they made their grief for their lord whom they saw follow the evil damsel. He and she come beneath the tree, and when they had come there, my lord Gauvain called to her:

"Maiden," says he, "now tell me if I can yet be quits; if it please you that I do more before I lose your favor, I shall do it, if ever I can."

The maiden said to him then: "Do you see now this deep ford, the banks of which are so high? My friend was wont to cross there when I wished, and went to gather for me some of the flowers that you see in those trees and on those meadows."

"Maiden, how did he cross there? I do not know where the ford is; the water is too deep, I fear, and the bank high everywhere, so that no one could go down to it."

"You would not dare enter it," says the maiden, "well do I know it. Never, certainly, did I think to myself that you would have enough heart to dare cross there; for that is the Perilous Ford, which no one, if he is not very courageous, dares pass for any pain."

Quickly my lord Gauvain brings his horse to the bank

and sees the deep water below and the steep bank above;
but the river was narrow. When my lord Gauvain sees
it, he says that his horse had leaped many a greater ditch
and thinks that he had heard it said and told in many
places that he who could cross the deep water of the
Perilous Ford would have all the renown in the world.
Then he goes away from the river and comes back in great
bounds to jump across, but he fails, for he did not take
his leap well, but jumped straight into the middle of the
ford. His horse swam until he took ground with four
feet, and fixed himself to jump, and he launches himself
so that he leaps on the bank, which is very high. When
he had come to the bank, he stood quite motionless on
his feet, for never could he stir; rather it behooved my
lord Gauvain to dismount by necessity, for he found his
horse very exhausted. He got down at once, and has a
desire to take off his saddle, and he has taken it off of
him and turned it on its side to dry it. When the girth
was taken off him he rubs down the water from his back
and sides and legs; then he puts on the saddle and mounts
up, and goes away at a slow walk until he saw a lone
knight who was hunting with a sparrow hawk. In the
meadow before the knight were three bird dogs. The
knight was more handsome than one could say by mouth.
When my lord Gauvain approaches him, he greeted him
and said to him:

"Fair lord, may that God who made you handsome
above any other creature give you today good fortune!"

He was quick to answer: "You are the good one,
you are the handsome one! But tell me, if it displease
you not, how you have left alone the evil maiden from
there? Where did her company go?"

"Lord," says he, "a knight, who bears a quartered
shield, was leading her when I encountered him."

"And what did you do with him?"

"I overcame him at arms."

"And what became of the knight?"

"The boatman has led him away, who said he was to have him."

"Certainly, fair lord, he told you true, and the maiden was my friend; but thus she was not that she ever wished to love me, nor did she deign to call me friend nor did I ever do her force, nor did I kiss her, this I pledge you, nor did she ever do my good; for I loved her against her will, for I took her from a friend of hers whom she was wont to lead with her, and I slew him and led her away and took pains to serve her. But my service was of no avail; for as soon as she could she sought opportunity to leave me and make her friend of that one from whom you have just now taken her, who was not a knight in jest, but was very worthy, so help me God, and yet he was never such that he ever dared to come into any place where he thought to find me. But you have today done such thing as no knight dare to do, and because you dare do it, you have conquered the renown of the world and its praise by your great prowess. When you leaped into the Perilous Ford, it came to you from great boldness, and know indeed truly that never did a knight come out of it."

"Lord," says he, "then the maiden lied to me, who told me and made me believe for true that her friend crossed it once a day for her love?"

"She said that, the renegade? Ha! would that she were now drowned in it, for she is very full of the devil! When she told you such a fable, she hates you, I can not deny it to you; and the devil, whom God confound, wanted to make you drown in the noisy and deep water! But now give me here your faith, and you will pledge to me, and I you: if you wish to ask me anything, whether it be my joy or my grief, that I shall not conceal the truth of it for anything, if I know it; and you also in turn will tell me anything that I shall wish to know, for never for anything will you lie to me about it, if you know how to tell me the truth of it."

They have both made this pledge, and my lord Gauvain begins to ask first:

"Lord," says he, "I ask you of a city that I see there, whose it is and what name it has?"

"Friend," says he, "of the city I shall tell the truth; for it is so fully mine that there is no man to whom I owe anything for it. I hold nothing of it except of God, and it is named Orquelenes."

"And what is your name?"

"Guiromelanz."

"Lord, you are very worthy and very valiant, I have heard it well said, and you are lord of a very great land. And what is the name of the maiden of whom no good news is told either near or far, as you bear witness of it?"

"I can indeed witness," says he, "that she does well to keep away; for she is too evil and disdainful, and for this she is named L'Orguelleuse de Logres, where she was born, and was brought from there as a little girl."

"And what is the name of her friend, who has gone, whether he wish to or not, into the prison of the boatman?"

"Friend, know of the knight that he is a marvelous knight and his name is Li Orguelleus de la Roche a l'Estroite Voie, who guards the ports of Galvoie."

"And what is the name of the castle, which is so very strong and fair, over there from where I came today, and where I ate yesterday evening and drank?"

At this word the Guiromelanz turned around as though grieving and begins to go away; and he begins to call him back:

"Lord, lord, speak to me, and remember your faith."

And the Guiromelanz stops, and turns completely around and says:

"May that hour that I saw you and that I pledged you my faith be shamed and accursed! Go away, I call it quits of your pledge. And do you release me from mine, for I believed to ask you some news of over there; but you know as much of the moon as you do of the castle, I believe."

"Lord," says he, "I lay there last night and I lay in the Bed of the Marvel, to which no bed is similar, nor did anyone ever see its equal."

"By my faith," says he, "I marvel much at the news that you say to me. Now it is a solace and delight for me to listen to your lies; for such would I hear a fabler tell as I do you: you are a jongleur, well do I see it. But I believed you were a knight and that you might have done some vassalage there. Nevertheless now tell me if you did any prowess there and what thing you saw there."

And my lord Gauvain said to him: "Lord, when I sat down on the bed, there was a very great storm in the palace, nor do I desire to lie to you about it. The cords of the bed creaked and some bells sounded, which hung to the cords of the bed. And the windows, which were closed, opened completely by themselves, and quarrels and polished arrows struck me on my shield, and the nails have remained there of a very fierce and crested lion, which had been long chained in a room. The lion was brought to me, for a villein let it go. The lion rushed toward me and struck at my shield so that it was held there by its nails so that it could not draw them out again. If you believe that it does not appear there, see the nails still here; for by God's mercy, I cut off its head and feet together. How do these tokens seem to you?"

The Guiromelanz at this word came to earth as quickly as he could, and he kneels and joins his hands and prays him that he pardon him the folly that he has said to him.

"I call it quits with you for it," says he, "but mount again."

And he remounts who has great shame for his folly and says: "Lord, if God keep me, I did not believe that anywhere, either near or far, there were to be for a hundred years he who might have the honor which has come to you. But of the white-haired queen, tell me if you know her and if you did not inquire of her who she is and whence she came."

"Never," says he, "did I remember it; but I saw her and I spoke to her."

"And I," says he, "shall tell it to you: she is the mother of King Arthur."

"By the faith that I owe God and His virtue, King Arthur, as I think, has not had a mother for a long time past, for he has indeed passed sixty years, to my knowledge, and much more."

"It is true, lord, she is his mother. When Uterpendragon his father was put in earth, it happened that the Queen Yguerne came to this country, and brought here all her treasure and established on that rock the castle and the palace as rich and beautiful as I have heard you describe. And you saw there, well do I know, the other queen, the other lady, the great, the beautiful, who was wife of king Lot and mother of that one who holds evil ways today: she is mother to Gauvain."

"Gauvain, fair lord, do I know well, and I dare indeed to say that that Gauvain has not had a mother for well twenty years past at least."

"Yes, he has, lord, never doubt it. After his mother

came there, burdened with a live child, with the very
beautiful, the very great damsel who is my friend, and
sister, I shall not conceal it from you, to that one to whom
God give great shame; for, truly, he would not carry
away his head, if I held him and I overcame him just as
I hold you here now; for I should cut it off for him on the
spot: nor would his sister aid him that I did not pull
his heart from his belly, I hate him so."

"You do not love as I do," says my lord Gauvain,
"by my soul: if I loved maiden or lady, for her love I
should love and serve all her lineage."

"You are right, well do I agree; but when I remember Gauvain, how his father slew mine, I can not wish
him any good; and he himself with his own hands slew,
of my cousins-german, a worthy and valiant knight. Never
could I come into a place to take vengeance on him in any
way. But now do me a service, if you go back to the
castle, that you will carry this ring to my friend and hand
it to her. I wish you to go there for me, and tell her that
I trust and believe so much in the love of her that she
would like better that her brother Gauvain should be
dead of bitter death than that I should have even the
smallest toe on my foot wounded. And you will greet
my friend for me and hand her this ring on behalf of me
who am her friend."

Then my lord Gauvain put the ring on his smallest
finger and says: "Lord, by the faith that I owe you, you
have a very courteous and wise friend, a gentle woman,
of high peerage, beautiful and gentle and debonair, if
she grant you this affair as you have told me here."

And he says: "Lord, you will do me great kindness,
this I grant you, if you carry my ring as a present to my
dear friend, for I love her much in great manner. And
I shall reward you, for of this castle I shall tell you the

name that you have asked me: the castle, if you do not
know it, is named the Roche de Chanpguin. Many a
good cloth both green and sanguine do they dye there,
and much is sold and bought there.

"Now have I told you that which pleased you, for
I have not lied to you by a word, and you in turn have told
me much good. Will you ask me anything else?"

"No, lord, except leave."

And he says: "Lord, you will tell me your name,
if it trouble you not, before I let you depart from me."

And my lord Gauvain says to him: "Lord, if the
Lord God help me, my name will never be concealed
from you; I am the one whom you hate so much: I am
Gauvain."

"You are Gauvain?"

"Truly, the nephew of King Arthur."

"By faith, you are then very bold or very foolish
to tell me your name, and you know that I hate you to
death. Now it annoys me and weighs upon me very
strongly that I do not have my helm laced and my shield
braced on my arm; for if I were armed as you are, know
this for certain, I should cut off your head right now,
for never should I leave it for anything. But if you
dared await me, I should go take my arms, then I should
come to fight you, and I should bring three or four men
to look at our battle; or, if you wish, let it go otherwise:
that we will wait for seven days and on the seventh day
we will come back to this place all armed, and you may
have sent word to the King and Queen and all her people,
and I shall have summoned my routs throughout all my
country, and our battle will not be made stealthily; rather
will all those see it who wish, for battle of such worthy
men as they say we two are ought not to be done in am-
bush; rather is it indeed right that many ladies and knights

be there. And when the one is wearied and all the world knows, the conqueror will have a thousand times more honor than he would have if no one but he knew it."

"Lord," says my lord Gauvain, "willingly would I forego, if it could be and should please you, that there should ever be a battle there; and if I have done anything wrong to you, quite willingly will I make amends for it through your friends and through mine so that it be right and good."

And he says: "I can not know what satisfaction there can be in that, if you do not dare fight me. I have described to you two things, so do whichever one you wish: if you dare, you will wait here for me and I shall go seek my arms, or you will summon from your land all your forces within seven days, for at Pentecost the court of King Arthur will be in Orcanie; well have I heard the news of it, not more than two days ago. Your messenger will be able to find there the King and his people prepared. Send there, and you will do wisely, for one day of respite is worth a hundred sous."

And he answers: "If God save me, the court will be there without any doubt. Know the whole truth of it, and I pledge you by my hand that I shall send there tomorrow or before my eyes close for sleep."

"Gauvain," says he, "and I wish to lead you to the best port in the world. This water is so swift and deep that nothing which may live can pass through it or leap to the other bank."

And my lord Gauvain answers: "Never shall I seek ford nor bridge there for anything that may happen to me. Rather than that the felonious damsel may hold it for baseness, I shall give her back her promise indeed, and so shall I go straight to her."

Then he spurs, and his horse leaped across the water swiftly, for he had no hindrance. When the maiden, who had attacked him so much by her speech, sees him cross toward her, she reined up her horse at the tree and came to him on foot, and she changed her heart and desire, so that she at once greets him and says that she has come to cry mercy for her misdeed, because he has endured great pain for her:

"Fair lord," says she, "now hear why I have been so arrogant toward all the knights in the world who have led me after them. I shall tell you, if it annoy you not. That knight, whom may God destroy, who spoke to you of me over there, badly employed his love on me, for he loved me, and I hated him; for he did me great annoyance that he slew, I shall not conceal it, him whose friend I was. Then he thought to do me so much honor that he thought to draw me to his love; but it never availed him anything, for the soonest that it was allowed me, I stole away from his company and joined the knight from whom you took me today, whom I don't value as much as a boot-strap. But of my first friend, when death parted me from him, I have so long been mad and so haughty of speech and so villainous, and so foolish that never did I take any care of whom I might be opposing, rather I did it knowingly because I wished to find one so ir-ritable that I might make him irritated and angered at me enough to cut me to pieces, for I have long wished to be slain. Fair lord, now take such justice of me that never more may maiden who hears the news of me dare say shame to any knight."

"Fair one," says he, "what does it amount to me that I do justice of you? Never may it please the Son of the Lord God that you have sorrow by me! But now mount, do not delay, and we will go to that strong castle. See the boatman at the port who is awaiting us to take us across."

"Your will from end to end will I do, lord," says the maiden.

Then she mounted into the saddle of the little shaggy palfrey, and they came to the boatman, who takes them across the water, for it was neither labor nor pain for him. The ladies see him coming, and the maidens, who had uttered very great grief for him; all the valets of the castle had also been out of their minds for him; now they have such joy that never again was any so great stirred up. In front of the palace the queen was seated to wait for him and she had had her maidens take hand in hand to dance and begin great joy. Against his coming they begin great joy, they sing and carol and dance, and he comes and dismounts among them. The ladies and the damsels and the two queens embrace him and speak to him with great joy, and with great festivity they disarm his legs and arms and feet and head. Of her whom he had brought they have also shown great joy, for all, men and women, served her for him, for they did nothing of it for her. With great joy they go into the palace and within it they all sat down. And my lord Gauvain has taken his sister and seated her beside him on the Bed of the Marvel, and says to her low and counsels her:

"Damsel, from beyond that port I bring you a ring of which the emerald is very green. A knight sends it to you by love and greets you and says that you are his love."

"Lord," says she, "I believe it indeed; but if I love him for anything, it is from afar that I am his friend, for never did he see me nor I him, except that I saw him across that water. But he has, by his mercy, given me his love long since, and he never came from there; but his messengers have prayed me so much that I have granted him my love, I would not lie about it; further than that I am not yet his friend."

"Ha! fair one, and yet he has boasted that you would much rather that my lord Gauvain, who is your brother-german, were dead than that he should have hurt in his toe."

"Ha! lord, much do I marvel how he said such great folly. By God, I did not believe that he was so badly trained. Now has he very badly protected himself who has sent me word of that thing. Alas! My brother does not know if I am born, nor did he ever see me. The Guiromelanz has spoken illy; for, by my soul, I should not wish his hurt more than my own."

While these two were talking thus, and the ladies were listening to them, the old queen sat down beside her daughter and said to her:

"Fair daughter, what does it seem to you of that lord who is seated beside your daughter, my grand-daughter? He has counseled her for a great while of I know not what, but it pleases me much, nor is it right that it grieve you, for it comes to him from great nobility when he holds to the fairest and to the wisest there is in this palace, and he is right. And would that it might please God that he had married her and that she might please him as much as Lavinia did Eneas!"

"Ha! lady," says the other queen, "may God give him so to put his heart that they be as brother and sister, and that he love her and she him so much that they both be one thing!"

In her prayer the lady intends that he love her and that he take her to wife; she does not recognize her son:

they will be like brother and sister, for there will be no other love there. When the one knows of the other that she is his sister and he her brother, his mother will have great joy other than she intends there. And my lord Gauvain has spoken so much to his sister, the fair one, that he gets up and calls a youth whom he saw on the right, the one who seemed to him to be most quick and worthy and helpful and wisest and most reasonable of all the youths in the hall. He goes down into a chamber and the youth alone with him. When they were both down, he said to him:

"Youth, I believe you very worthy, very wise, and very cunning. If I tell you a counsel of mine, I advise you to conceal it very well in order that you may have advantage from it. I wish to send you to a place where great joy will be made you."

"Lord, I should rather have my tongue torn out of my throat than that a single word should have flown from my mouth that you should wish concealed."

"Brother," says he, "then you will go to my lord the King Arthur, for my name is Gauvain, his nephew. The way is not long or difficult, for in the city of Orcanie has the King established to hold his court at the Pentecost. And if the way costs you anything that far, rely upon me for it. When you come before the King, you will find him very angered. And when you greet him on my behalf, he will have very great joy; indeed there will not be a single one who hears the news who will not be glad of it. To the King you will say, faith that he owes me, for he is my lord, and I his man, that he fail not for any occasion that I find him not before the fifth day of the feast lodged down the meadow beneath this tower, and let there be there such company of high people and of low, as shall have come to his court; that I have undertaken battle against a knight who prizes neither me nor him as scarcely of any worth; it is the Guiromelanz without fail, who hates me with mortal hatred. Likewise you will tell the Queen that she come here by the great faith which must be between her and me, for she is my lady and my friend; and she will not leave it off, as soon as she knows the news, and let her for my love bring here the ladies and the maidens who are at her court that day. But of one thing I have great fear: that you may not have such a hunter that may quickly carry you that far."

And he answers him that he has one large and swift and strong and good, that he will lead as his own.

"This," says he, "does not trouble me."

And the youth quickly leads him toward a stable and takes from it and brings strong and fresh hunters, one of which was ready to ride and to travel, for he had had it newly shod, nor did it lack saddle or bridle.

"By faith," says my lord Gauvain, "youth, you are well provided. Now go, may the Lord of kings give you to go and come well and to hold the straight way!"

Thus he sends the youth away and escorts him to the water and commands the boatman to help him cross over. The boatman helped him pass, for never did it behoove him to linger, for he had rowers enough. The youth has passed beyond, and toward the city of Orcanie he has chosen the straight way, for if anyone knows how to ask the way he can go throughout the world.

My lord Gauvain returns to his palace, where he sojourns in great joy and great delight, for they all love him and serve him there. And the queen had baths heated in five hundred tubs, and had all the youths enter them to bathe. And robes had been appointed for them which were made ready when they had come out of the bath. The cloths were woven with gold, and the linings were of ermine.   At the minster, until after Matins the youths kept vigil on foot, for never did they kneel there.   In the morning my lord Gauvain with his own hands put on each the right spur and girded on the sword and gave him the accolade.   Then he had company of at least five hundred new knights.

The youth went until he came to the city of Orcanie, where the King was holding such court as befitted the day. And the lame and the wolf-diseased, who go looking at the youth, say:

"This one comes in great need.   I believe that he brings from afar great news to the court.   Much will he find the King both mute and deaf, whatever he can say; for he is very full of grief and ire.   And who will know how to give counsel when he has heard from the messenger how it is?"

"Come on!" say they others, "how does it concern us to speak of the King's counsel?   You should be in fright and dismayed and bewildered when we have lost that one who for God dressed us all, and from whom all good things came to us through alms and charity."

Thus through all the city the poor people who loved him much regretted my lord Gauvain.   And the youth passes by, and has gone until he found the King sitting in his palace, around him a hundred counts palatine and a hundred dukes and a hundred kings seated.   The King was mournful and pensive when he saw his great barony and saw nothing of his nephew, and he falls in a faint through great distress.   In lifting him up, the one who could come there first was without laziness, for all run to sustain him.   My lady Lore was sitting in a bower, and heard the grief that was made in the hall.   She goes down from the bower, and came to the Queen just like one bewildered. And when the Queen sees her, she asks her what was the matter with her. . . .

Explycit Percevax le viel

SELECTED BIBLIOGRAPHY

A. Texts

Chrestien de Troyes, *Der Percevalroman (Li Contes del Graal),* *unter Benutzung des von G. Baist nachgelassen handschriftlichen Materials,* ed. Alfons Hilka. Halle, 1932.

———— *Li Contes del Graal,* ed. William Roach. Genève, 1950.

———— *Perceval le Gallois,* tr. Lucien Foulet. Paris, 1947.

———— *Arthurian Romances,* tr. W. W. Comfort. London, n.d.

Gerbert de Montreuil, *La Continuation de Perceval,* ed. Mary Williams. Paris, 1922-25.

Le Haut Livre du Graal, Perlesvaus, ed. W. A. Nitze. Chicago, 1932-37. 2 vols.

The Mabinogion. London, n.d.

La Queste del Saint Graal, ed. A. Pauphilet. Paris, 1923.

Roach, William, *The Didot-Perceval.* Philadelphia, 1941.

Roach, William, *et al.,* eds., *The Continuations of the Old French Perceval of Chrétien de Troyes.* Philadelphia, 1949-52. 3 vols.

Robert de Boron, *Le Roman de l'Estoire dou Graal,* ed. W. A. Nitze, Paris, 1927.

Sir Perceval of Gales. The Camden Society, 1844.

Vulgate Version of the Arthurian Romances, ed. H. O. Sommer. Washington, 1909-16. 8 vols.

Wolfram von Eschenbach, *The Parzival,* tr. E. H. Zeydel and B. Q. Morgan. Chapel Hill, 1951.

B. Studies

Anderson, Lady Flavia, *The Ancient Secret.* London, 1953.

Frappier, Jean, *Chrétien de Troyes, l'homme et l'oeuvre.* Paris, 1957.

Guyer, Foster E., *Chrétien de Troyes.* New York, 1957.

Hofer, Stefan, *Chrétien de Troyes, Leben und Werk.* Köln, 1954.

Holmes, U. T., Jr., *History of Old French Literature.* Chapel Hill, 1937; New York, 1948.

———— and Klenke, Sister M. A., *Chrétien, Troyes, and the Grail.* Chapel Hill, 1959.

Loomis, R. S., *Arthurian Tradition and Chrétien de Troyes.* New York, 1949.

———— *Celtic Myth and Arthurian Romance.* New York, 1927.

———— *Arthurian Literature in the Middle Ages,* New York, 1959.

Marx, Jean, *La Légende Arthurienne et le graal.* Paris, 1951.

Parry, J. J., *Arthurian Bibliography.* New York, Modern Language Association of America, 1931. Continued in *Modern Language Quarterly,* with Margaret Slauch, 1940 ff.

Pope, Arthur U., "Persia and the Holy Grail," *The Literary Review,* I (1957), 57-71.

Reinhard, J. R., *Chrétien de Troyes, a Bibliographical Essay.* Ann Arbor, 1932.

Séchelles, D. de, *L'Origine du Graal.* Saint-Brieuc, 1954.

Unger, Max, "The Cradle of the Parzifal Legend," *Musical Quarterly,* XVIII (1912), 428-42.

Weston, Jessie L., *The Legend of Sir Percival.* London, 1909.